INSIDE
OUTWARD
BOUND

INSIDE OUTWARD BOUND

Renate Wilson

The East Woods Press

Charlotte, North Carolina

The East Woods Press
Fast & McMillan Publishers, Inc.
820 East Boulevard
Charlotte, North Carolina   28203

ISBN 0-914788-41-8
Library of Congress Catalog Card Number 81-65475

The chapter "From Crowd to Community" was extracted from the article "Outward Bound . . . Rolling with the Punch," by Elaine Dickinson, in *Sail,* January 1976, with kind permission.

Cover design by Nancy Legue
Printed and bound in Canada by D.W. Friesen & Sons Ltd.

This book is for Hugh,
who is always outward bound.

Contents

Acknowledgements

I would like to thank the many Outward Bound people who assisted me with the preparation of this book. In particular, I am grateful to Ray Preece and Art Rogers for their unfailing helpfulness; Josh and Mrs. Miner, Ulf Händel and Derek Prithard for a great deal of information and very welcome hospitality; Peter Willauer who made my Solo on Ohio Island possible, and Wendy Pieh for her instant friendship. And I cannot forget those who led me: Lonnie Nicholls, through the swamp, Rolf Mantler up the rocks, Tino O'Brien over the ropes course, and Matty McNair through the rapids shouting "Smile, Renate, smile" as I grimly paddled my kayak.

My thanks also to Lola Hahn for giving me a glimpse into Kurt Hahn's life; Cornelia Hahn Oberlander for allowing me to read letters written to Hahn's family on his death; Wendy Johnson, who kindly reproduced the historical photographs provided by Capt. F. Fuller, and Margaret Campbell, who wielded a razor-sharp but always constructive editor's pencil.

I went into the woods because I wished to live deliberately,
to confront the essential facts of life, and to see
if I could not learn what it had to teach, and not,
when I came to die, discover that I had not lived.

Henry David Thoreau

Chapter 1
From Crowd to Community

I stood with 170 other anxious young people in the rain on the ferry pier in Rockland, Maine. We nervously awaited the first instructions that would mark the beginning of a 26-day course at the Hurricane Island Outward Bound School. We had come from every part of the United States, from wealthy suburbs and from big city ghettos on scholarships. Some of us had come to see Maine. Some to see the ocean for the first time. And others to learn how to sail. But beyond these reasons each of us had come to answer a vague challenge—a personal challenge not yet understood or appreciated.

Standing in the cold rain I studied the tense faces around me. Each face expressed varying degrees of skepticism, bewilderment and downright fear. We suffered from nagging doubts about why we were there and why we were offering ourselves up to a mysterious adventure called Outward Bound. . . . But as the weather worsened, it was difficult to think profound thoughts and philoso-phize.

From that moment on I forgot my abstract speculation. I was swept up with the other students into the total learning experience of Outward Bound: to learn by doing. Students were quickly divided into "watches" of 12. Although most students are based on Hurricane Island, two other islands, Bartlett Island and Burnt Island, are used for the course. . . . My watch of 12 women was assigned to Burnt Island, 20 miles south. . . . The first of many Outward Bound surprises came when we were told that we were to sail there that afternoon in spite of the rainy, stormy weather. . . .

At the dock we each were issued a lifejacket, foul-weather gear, boots, a duffle bag, a plastic tarp, a journal, a knife and whistle and 20 feet of string. From that day on Carson Watch (named after writer Rachel Carson) lived, worked, ate and slept together. . . . Most of us knew nothing about sailing or even how to row. . . . Our instructors, Liza Cocroft and Bob Weiler, immediately crammed a multitude of information into our heads as we awk-wardly scurried about the boat trying to follow directions and appear to know what we were doing. . . . Bob and Liza relentlessly prodded and guided us as we fumbled our way away from the dock. Our boat, Blue Heron, *and two boats of our companion men's watches,* Sinbad *and* Queequeg, *set sail shakily in rain and strong winds for [uninhabited] Burnt Island.*

Our boat was a pulling boat—it was a converted 30-foot lifeboat with four rowing positions on each side. She was ketch-rigged and had no winches—everything we did such as hoisting sails, lower-ing or pulling up the centerboard, shipping the rudder and trimm-ing the mainsheet took sheer muscle power. We had very few muscles among us at first. . . . We felt intimidated by the harsh weather and our own weakness.

At first the daily routine [on Burnt Island] was unbearable. We rose at 5:00 AM, . . . ran the island's coastal trail (3½ miles) and then jumped off the pier into the icy water. I jumped without breaking my trot from the trail mainly because I was too tired and wretched to care what I did next—a dynamic new concept in waking up. . . .

"We ate and slept sardine-style aboard our beloved vessel."
(Hurricane Island Outward Bound School)

Projects ranged from sailing practice, boat maintenance, trail building, knot-tying lessons, and first-aid instruction, to rappelling and climbing the island's 30- to 70-foot cliffs. . . . Most of my watch resisted the exhausting pace and met each new assignment with complaints, tears and exasperation. . . . After a week of unbearable constant physical and mental exertion it dawned on me that this was Outward Bound. As personal everyday habits became irrelevant I forced myself to adopt this new lifestyle—roll with the punch, as it were. . . . After I adopted this fatalistic philosophy I was delighted to find the daily pace easier to take and soon exhilarating.

Every night we assigned a boat watch in which two students took one-hour shifts. To me it meant I would be dragged out of my warm sleeping bag into the cold, pitch-dark morning at some deathly hour such as 3:00 or 4:00. Although the discipline of boat watch was good for us (so they said), on expedition we anchored in rocky, unknown waters and the low tides continually presented problems. Boat watch was then essential to our safety.

Under sail each girl took turns at various sailing jobs: helmsman, navigator, bow watch, manning the sheets, dropping anchor, docking. At first each student was petrified to take over an unfamiliar position, such as the helm. Helmsman had to take charge, give orders and make all the decisions. . . . Peer pressure at its ultimate, no one could be a passenger on Blue Heron. *After a quick briefing we were thrown into each task and left to our own resources and judgment. . . . We ate and slept sardine-style aboard our beloved vessel. Twelve women wrung out from a day of sailing getting settled for a few hours sleep on oars [laid across the thwarts] get acquainted in no time.*

The ultimate test . . . came on the last afternoon of training expedition. . . . We were instructed to anchor on a treeless, grassless rock ledge. . . . Liza announced, "OK Carson Watch, this is a shipwreck drill! You have one minute to get off the boat with six things which have to include water jugs, exposure kit and first-aid pack." Like fools we shrugged and thought of how much trouble it was going to be to drag all that gear and food off the boat only to put it back on board again. After we had blithely hopped off onto rocks, Bob and Liza pulled in the line and sailed away . . . as we stared in disbelief.

Naturally we were distraught at being abandoned without warm clothes or food on a pile of rocks in the ocean covered with nothing but seagull droppings. But this drill was our most important lesson—we had not reacted to Liza's command in a serious or realistic manner. Going hungry for one night taught us more than any lecture about priorities and fast action. On a lighter side this "shipwreck" afforded Carson Watch our first real opportunity to sit down together and talk. The night was a long, cold one and we finally got to know each other. . . .

Prior to our first sailing expedition we had been a rather blundering and disorganized group of individuals, waiting to be led by the hand through the Outward Bound sailing course. It was now obvious that the burden of learning to sail lay upon each of us and we showed more initiative in thinking and acting together, and in giving and taking orders from each other. We progressively became more alert and decisive and confident enough to man and navigate a 30-foot sailboat in unfamiliar waters with safety and, later, a great deal of pleasure. . . .

The contrast between [our final five-day expedition] and our first expedition was a pleasant revelation. . . . Students were in complete charge of this trip. By now we knew exactly what preparations we needed to make—organizing meals, packing food, taking boat inventory and consolidating duffle bags. We could plan any route we wished and organize ourselves in whatever manner worked best.

As Expedition Navigator for Carson Watch, I met with the navigators [of the other two boats in our convoy] and we planned a course. . . . Each morning we held a captain's and navigator's meeting to study the charts and plan that day's rendezvous points, where the three watches would confirm or change courses for the next destination. In contrast to our training expedition we were no longer afraid to take responsibility. Previously shy individuals were asserting themselves. Manning Blue Heron *was easier than* we ever imagined with most of us in top physical condition by now. . . .

Blue Heron's *final sail back to Burnt [Island] was in dense fog—the first cloudy weather we had since the first two days of the course. By now we were a weathered, sun-tanned group of women. We were aware and sorry that this would be the last time we'd sail together—as friends, as Carson Watch and as Outward Bound. . . .*

The night before we were to be bused to Boston to disappear back into our former lives, Bob and Liza ordered Carson Watch to prepare for a night sail in the fog. We almost believed them, but realized they wanted us out on Blue Heron *to say goodbye. We each sat in silence in the same position we had occupied that first day in Rockland and thought about how far we had come. We were an intimate group of strangers who had shared every imaginable emotion. Carson Watch was about to disperse forever back into the real world. But at that moment nothing was real to us but our boat, the sounds of the water around us and the bond of our common experience. . . .*

We left the island with barely a trace of our presence. Burnt Island remained as unchanged as the ocean around it. Not one student could say the same. . . .

Elaine Dickinson, in *Sail,* January 1976

Chapter 2
A Builder of Bandwagons

Few of the women on *Blue Heron* were aware how much they owed to the idealism of a Central-European Jewish intellectual. They were responding to the adventure, the challenge, the sense of self-discovery that is part of Outward Bound; they were benefiting from the vision of a man whose passion for teaching young people, together with his imagination and generous heart, had resulted in a unique approach to education. His name was Kurt Hahn and he was without a doubt a genius.

When Kurt Hahn first visited the United States, the immigration officer asked him what he did for a living.

"I build bandwagons," replied Hahn.

Outward Bound was his most successful and enduring bandwagon.

Kurt Hahn was born in Berlin in 1886 and lived to be eighty-eight years old. He grew up in a wealthy Jewish home where gracious living went hand in hand with heated political discussion, and academic excellence was taken for granted. His parents held open house for politicians, artists and scholars as well as industrialists. His father, Oskar, travelled widely on behalf of the family steel business, and the country he most loved to visit was England. When he died, Kurt was just eighteen but by then had inherited his father's love of everything English. After some years at Göttingen University, he went to England in 1910 to continue his studies in Philosophy and the Classics at Oxford.

Like his mother, Charlotte, Kurt became convinced that the good in everyone could be awakened and developed by the right environment and teaching. To his younger brothers and their many friends, he was a protector and guiding spirit.

Kurt Hahn had a talent for attracting people and establishing an easy rapport with them. Most of those who met him became admirers, and helpers in his numerous projects. Many of his friendships led directly to creating Outward Bound. For instance, a visit to the home of a fellow student at Oxford, William (later Sir William) Calder, introduced him to the Moray coast of Scotland that was to become the setting for his first educational experiment in the United Kingdom twenty years later. While Hahn was convalescing from surgery in the Calder home in 1913, he drew up a plan for a new kind of school. A visitor there was the German educator Karl Reinhard, who made a half-serious promise to be director of studies if Hahn's dream ever materialized, a promise he was called on to make good just seven years later. The theories of education that the two men discussed would contribute much to the final form of Outward Bound.

Another youthful friendship may well have saved Hahn's life. A young Englishman, Neville Butler, caught in Berlin during World War I, was befriended by the Hahn family. When Kurt was imprisoned by the Nazis in 1933, Butler, by then secretary to the British Prime Minister Ramsay MacDonald, helped secure his release.

When Air Vice Marshall Sir Lawrence Darvell, commandant of the NATO Staff Training College in France after the war, told Hahn how well even former enemies were working together at the college, Hahn's imagination was fired. The result was the first United World College, which opened in Wales in 1962. Here students from many countries complete the last two years of high school together, studying in an atmosphere of international co-operation that hopefully influences both their ideas and their careers. The International Convention on Life Saving Techniques held in 1960 grew out of a conversation between Hahn and Sir Adrian Curlewis, who was active in the Surf Life Saving Association of Australia. Talks with high-ranking members of the British medical establishment led to the Medical Commission on Accident Prevention. Through his friendship with the Greek Royal Family (both King Konstantin and Prince Philip were his students) Hahn was able to help in the repatriation of 5,000 Greek children after World War II.

But his most fruitful relationship was with Prince Max von Baden, the last imperial chancellor of Germany whose secretary Hahn had become towards the end of World War I. In 1920 von Baden offered Hahn a wing of his ancestral home, the huge Schloss Salem near Lake Constance, for the kind of school he had mapped out in his sickroom on the Moray coast. With Hahn as headmaster, the Prince as "working patron" and Karl Reinhard as director of studies, Salem developed into one of the most famous schools in Europe and became a model for several others.

Hahn and von Baden admitted adapting educational principles from many sources—from Plato, from Sparta in its heyday, from Lord Baden-Powell, the founder of the Boy Scouts, and from the British public school system. In some ways they were ahead of their time: Prince Max spoke about caring for the environment nearly half a century before the word ecology became commonplace.

Salem was the antithesis of the authoritarian German

Kurt Hahn, builder of bandwagons
(Capt. F. Fuller)

schools. The students were "put on their honour"—in other words, their word was guarantee of their having carried out certain obligations—and they were encouraged to follow their own conscience instead of being constantly supervised. They were required to give some sort of service to the school community, though a few youngsters treated this requisite lightly—one boy chose as his job the watering of a cactus which only had to be done once a month!

The principle of equality was taken seriously. Hahn felt that the children of the rich and powerful had to be "emancipated from the prison of privilege" and he encouraged his students to trade their labour for provisions from the local farmers and to learn craftsmanship from local artisans. Poorer children, on the other hand, had to be rescued from "inequality of opportunity," so fees were on a sliding scale and parents were assessed what they could afford. Some even paid with heirlooms rather than money. Golo Mann, son of the author Thomas Mann, remembers paying ten American dollars for one whole term. Slow learners and children with learning disabilities were as welcome as the academically bright, girls as readily as boys.

In such an atmosphere, the teachers, too, had to learn new ways. When one of them said at a teachers' conference, "I don't have any confidence in this child," he was told by Karl Reinhard, "In that case, you have no right to teach him."

Kurt Hahn used to say that the boys of Salem School were known wherever they went, not by their intellectual achievements, considerable as those might be, nor by their physical prowess, distinguished as this often was, but by the gleam in their eyes. Therein is the best clue to the kind of student Hahn wanted to emerge from his school.

When Hitler became chancellor of Germany in 1933, the school and its Jewish cofounder were doomed. The principles of truthfulness, freedom of expression, justice, and love for others practised at Salem were incompatible with Nazism. When a gang of young Nazis kicked a Communist youth to death before his mother's eyes, and were congratulated for their action by Hitler himself, Hahn sent a message to all former students of Salem challenging them to break any ties they might have with the Nazis. The Gestapo imprisoned him in 1933 after the Nazis' total takeover of Germany. He was released with the help of his old friend Neville Butler, and went straight to the Moray Firth where he had regained his health twenty years before.

Hahn must have made a strange picture as he strode the Scottish beaches and hills: a tall man with a large, almost bald head who, because of a painful allergy to bright sunlight, wore big, floppy hats and voluminous clothes. He was now nearly fifty years old, and had no home, no job and little money, but he had an abundance of ideas and friends.

On one of his long walks he discovered the large but neglected castle of Gordonstoun, now standing vacant. Hahn took his find as a good omen. Once before he had helped convert a great building into a school; he would do so again. Soon he was engaged in a flurry of activity. He promoted his idea among his numerous friends, gave a series of lectures, obtained a loan of £1,000 and took a lease on Gordonstoun. When the school opened its doors in 1934 it differed in just about every respect from other British "public" schools (which are, of course, private schools). It had no history, no tradition, little money and a very special curriculum. Although only thirteen boys were enrolled, one of them lent immediate stature to the school: Prince Philip of Greece, whose older sister had married Max von Baden's son and who had been a student at Salem for a short time.

That which had worked so well at Salem was transplanted to Gordonstoun and added to the normal academic curriculum. So, for instance, students were encouraged to improve their athletic standards by working alone against a yardstick and a stopwatch. As with so many of Hahn's ideas, this one did not originate with him but with a man he much admired, Dr. Bernhard Zimmermann, head of the Institute of Physical Education

Gordonstoun: a neglected castle when discovered by Kurt Hahn, now a school famous throughout the world

(Gordonstoun School)

at Göttingen University. Dr. Zimmermann had developed a system whereby steadily increasing demands are made on the body through graduated exercises. An athlete could start at virtually any level and improve his performance by the daily execution of a number of activities. When Dr. Zimmermann, too, became a refugee in Britain, Hahn quickly recruited him for Gordonstoun. Unlike most sports coaches, he was much more interested in the average or poor athlete than the good one. This fitted Hahn's own belief that each child must be helped to achieve goals within his own abilities and that everyone can improve given the motivation, the encouragement and the opportunity to do so.

Hahn loved games but disliked professional sports. Competition was fine, he believed, as long as it was not taken too seriously and was scrupulously fair, with no side having a definite advantage. "We must dethrone games," he told his teachers. Once, when an opposing team in a track meet were preparing to compete barefoot because they could not afford running shoes, Hahn ordered his students to play without their shoes. When the young American teacher Josh Miner introduced to the school a new and much more successful method of high jumping, Hahn insisted that the old style should be kept so that no one gained advantage because of technique. Only much later did Miner understand what Hahn was getting at when he said, "Josh, we want to develop people through jumping, not make jumpers out of people."

Vigorous exercise, Hahn believed, would carry boys through the stressful period of puberty, a time of great temptation, great trial, great passions. *Leidenschaft,* or "passion," was a word Hahn used continually in his writing, conversation and speeches. "Good passions" meant physical fitness, intellectual curiosity, helping your neighbour, adhering to truth and justice under all circumstances. "Bad" ones included sloth, greed, passivity in the face of adversity, selfishness. At Gordonstoun, as at Salem, the emphasis was on fostering the "good passions."

One of Kurt Hahn's favourite readings from the Bible was the story of the Good Samaritan, and he applied the lesson of helping one's neighbour at Gordonstoun. The school was shaped by its proximity to the sea, and maintained its own fleet of small boats and the larger training ship *Prince Louis*. The little harbour of Hopeman became an extension of the school's playing fields. It was inevitable that Gordonstoun should become part of the coast guard network, the boys supplying round-the-clock watchers during bad weather. The school's Fire Service, too, became part of the local fire department, and its Mountain Rescue Service brought in many an exhausted, lost or injured hiker.

Early in his career as a teacher, Hahn had realized that young people need a recognizable mark of achievement. At Gordonstoun, he introduced a system of badges. Boys could earn a badge by a combination of athletic accomplishment, an extended sea or land expedition, working alone on a long-term project, and some form of service to the community. The Gordonstoun Badge was renamed Moray Badge when it was extended to boys from the surrounding communities, and later was broadened to the County Badge. Once boys from outside the school were invited to compete for badges, another requirement was added—to refrain from smoking and drinking during the training period for the badge. Today the Duke of Edinburgh Award can be earned by young people anywhere in the British Commonwealth for completing roughly the same set of tasks as developed at Gordonstoun. And at related Outward Bound schools all over the world, badges are awarded upon successful completion of the Standard Course.

When war broke out in 1939, the Moray Firth was considered to be in the path of a possible German invasion. Gordonstoun School was evacuated to Wales, and its "instant traditions" went with it, ready now to become incorporated into Outward Bound, another bandwagon which Hahn would put his heart and soul into building.

Kurt Hahn had hundreds of friends and acquaintances, but no two of them agree about his personality apart from his greatness in illuminating the path they travelled together, whether they worked with him for years or only enjoyed a few hours of conversation with him. No one seems to bear him ill will, not even those whose encounters resulted in fierce argument or implacable differences of opinion, or who experienced Hahn's occasional bad manners, such as the time he disappeared from a breakfast meeting, leaving his guest to wait patiently for several hours before discovering that his host had left for the airport without explanation.

To his students, he was at once inspiring and intimidating, as Prince Georg Wilhelm of Hanover remembers: "I think each one of us was at first somewhat overpowered by the strong rays of his personality, his searching eyes which tried to ascertain whether we had a spark in us that could be ignited. But this anxious moment was bridged by the obvious kindness he was able to transmit."

Hahn took a personal interest in each of his pupils; he observed them carefully and was an excellent judge of character. Of the Queen's future husband he wrote: "Prince Philip is a born leader, but will need the exacting demands of a great service to do justice to himself. His best is outstanding—his second best is not good enough."

Much of what Hahn stood for was misunderstood, misinterpreted or misquoted. Josh Miner, who taught at Gordonstoun and later helped to bring Outward Bound to the United States, admits ruefully that it is sometimes difficult to distinguish between what Hahn actually said, what he was reported to have said, what other people said about him, and what would have been nice had he said. One thing on which everyone agrees was his flair for the English language. After the holocaust which had its roots in Germany, he said that "the fault did not lie in the badness of the wicked, but in the weakness of the good." Disappointed in a candidate for teaching seamanship at Gordonstoun, he complained: "I was looking for a bluff naval officer; you sent me a cantankerous sea official." Gordonstoun teachers were told that bad teaching techniques could be compared to "pouring and pouring into a jug and never looking to see whether the lid is off." He described preaching to young people as "a hook without a worm," and argued that the best way to teach was to "impel students into experience"—an expression that has found its way into Outward Bound terminology. Hahn encouraged his students to recognize their own worth, or to "eliminate the misery of unimportance." He was heard to mutter that "some parents negotiate with their children as if they were a foreign power." Although he demanded much of himself and his colleagues, he was tolerant of human weakness. "Human nature is very prevalent" was one of his favourite expressions.

It was certainly "very prevalent" in his own life, which encompassed so many apparent contradictions that even his firmest admirers found some of them difficult to reconcile. He loved England passionately, and he loved the country of his birth, though they had fought two bitter wars against each other in his lifetime. At the same time he believed himself to be a *Weltbürger*: a citizen of the world. Although to the end of his days he remained what he was at the beginning—a Central-European intellectual, proud of being a Jew—he nevertheless became a member of the Church of England and was baptized in Liverpool Cathedral. He was at times a shrewd businessman who could charm large sums out of the most tightly closed fist, yet he had little actual money sense and was quite capable of giving a New York taxi driver ten dollars for a short trip and waving away the change. He was an ardent pacifist, but thought that young people need the "moral equivalent of war" to bring out the best in them.

A great congregation of friends, former colleagues and pupils gathered at Schloss Salem in 1966 to celebrate Kurt Hahn's eightieth birthday. There were many speeches but the best and by far the longest one was made by the celebrant himself. The old fires were hardly dimmed by age, the memory faltered only occasionally, and deep concern for youth shone through every word. Many of the same people paid tribute again eight years later at Hahn's funeral services, which were held at Salem, in London and at Gordonstoun.

The Duke of Edinburgh had this to say of his former headmaster: "Eccentric perhaps, innovator certainly, great beyond doubt."

Chapter 3
An Idea Responds to a Need

The birth of Outward Bound was the result of Kurt Hahn's bringing together the right people with the right ideas at precisely the right time.

Perhaps the most influential of these was Lawrence Holt, a member of the shipping family that owned the Blue Funnel Line. He had been a magistrate, city councillor and lord mayor of Liverpool, and sat on several commissions to improve employment conditions for dockers and miners. Not content to work only at these levels, he also did personal service in boys' clubs and dockside missions. He was a rich man who used his money to many good purposes. One of these was a contribution towards a scholarship at Gordonstoun, the school to which he sent his son Julian. In another move to aid the school, he seconded officers from the Holt company to supervise a school-boy crew sailing the training ship *Prince Louis* from Scotland to

Gordonstoun's wartime home in Wales.

Lawrence Holt mourned the passing of the great sailing ships, not so much for romantic reasons as for the very practical one that modern steamships do not require the same degree of seamanship from their crews as do sailing vessels. When German submarines began to attack British ships, the truth became shockingly clear: the younger sailors in both the Merchant and the Royal Navy seemed to be far less capable of surviving a torpedoing than the old salts. Large steel ships with sophisticated equipment had shielded them from the vagaries of the sea; they didn't know how to navigate lifeboats and rafts; most important of all, they were dying for lack of will to survive in the face of extreme hardships. Part of the reason was that these young sailors came from a population generally weakened by years of depression. They were therefore physically unable to withstand the rigours of hours or days in lifeboats or clinging to wreckage in the middle of the icy, heaving North Sea and Atlantic. But part of the problem, too, was that they simply lacked the toughness and resourcefulness of the more experienced sailors. Holt viewed their deaths with despair and a quiet fury.

Kurt Hahn and Lawrence Holt complemented each other beautifully. Hahn was gregarious, voluble, infectiously enthusiastic, a visionary and "idea man" who brushed obstacles aside, convinced that more practical souls would overcome them to further his plans. Holt was a gentle giant of a man, diffident and self-effacing, a doer rather than a talker. Both men shared a great concern for young people, and answered with a loud "Yes" the question "Are you your brother's keeper?"

The two men met when Hahn's fortunes were at a low ebb. In 1940 Gordonstoun was struggling to keep going in the makeshift quarters at Plas Dynam, Wales, to which the school had been evacuated. The County Badge scheme, which Hahn had wanted to make country-wide, had not caught on as well as he had hoped. He had found a house for a possible residential centre where young people could combine a holiday with working towards the Badge, but he had no money to buy or even rent it. Jim Hogan, the young schoolmaster whom he had briefly met, liked, and decided to make warden of such a centre, was skeptical that it would ever become a reality.

In one of Hahn's characteristic flashes of inspiration, he sent Jim Hogan to Liverpool to talk to Lawrence Holt. Hogan told him of the County Badge plan, and of "Bryneithin," the grey stone building, perched above the ever-changing vista of high and low tide in the Dovey estuary, that Hahn had already picked out. The County Badge scheme not only made sense to Holt but seemed to offer just the sort of training he thought young sailors needed to prepare them for seagoing duty. Then and there he decided to buy the house and to lend trained seamen to teach seamanship. He would send eight cadets from his company and persuade the officer commanding the training ship H.M.S. *Conway* to make an equal number of his cadets available. Gordonstoun was to supply eight of their boys, as well as instructors for all aspects of training except the nautical ones. These twenty-four boys would start the first course at the Aberdovey Sailing School in five weeks' time.

It is fascinating to see how the decisions made then formed the basis for what was shortly to become Outward Bound. Determining the length of the course was the first important step. Gordonstoun had already experimented with two- and three-week summer programs for working lads, young soldiers and National Fire Service dispatch riders, but these shorter courses had not seemed to succeed in making a lasting impression on the mostly city folk. Hardly any of them were in good enough physical shape to keep up with the schoolboys on distance runs; they smoked heavily, and were afraid to be outdoors by themselves. But they did go away in better condition than when they arrived, and Hahn had taken note of this: for the Aberdovey school, a period of twenty-eight days was thought to be the shortest time in which real improvement could be achieved and the longest time that the cadets might be expected to be given leave to attend.

In the beginning, Aberdovey was a sea school. Here, cadets muster for morning parade.

(Capt. F. Fuller)

Prince Philip inspecting officers at Aberdovey

(Capt. F. Fuller)

Both Hahn and Holt saw the urgent need to find ways of increasing the stamina of the boys. Before the youngsters came to Aberdovey, few of them had ever done more than play soccer on a meadow or "catch" on a city street. Encouraged by the infectious enthusiasm of Dr. Zimmermann, who was borrowed from Gordonstoun, they learned to throw a javelin, discus and shotput, to do long and high jumps, to run and sprint and, above all, to climb and walk long distances in the rugged Welsh hills. Towards the end of the twenty-eight days even the weediest were sent on cross-country hikes of up to thirty miles, climbing a couple of peaks on the way. This regime was not adopted without some misgivings. Jim Hogan writes of being much concerned with the danger of straining the boys. Before Dr. Zimmermann came to Salem, boys there were told not to cycle uphill! His training methods demonstrated that every youngster could improve his athletic performance, no matter how inexperienced he was in a sport, and that he would not be harmed by the effort.

To the toughening regime of athletics, hiking, and rowing and sailing open boats was added a strict nonsmoking and nondrinking rule, and better meals were provided than the boys had got at home in the years before the war. The formula was to prove successful.

Aberdovey was a sea school. The boys were issued a simple uniform of navy blue jersey and pants. Naval terminology, inspection of quarters, marching in formation, morning prayers, flag raising, and "sir-ing" of officers were the order of the day. Much of the training was carried out in small boats and in the *Prince Louis.*

One problem encountered by seamen who had been torpedoed was getting into lifeboats and rafts from their badly listing or sinking ships. Invariably this meant entrusting their lives to a flapping rope or net dangling above the heaving sea. To prepare boys for this eventuality, a ropes obstacle course was constructed in a grove of trees on the school grounds. It consisted of thick hawsers suspended from the higher branches, rope ladders, a "Burma bridge" of three ropes strung between two trees, fixed and wobbly logs suspended between ropes and treetrunks, slings to swing on and nets to land in. A smooth wall approximated the side of a ship or a dock, and climbing it taught the boys the value of teamwork since no one could get over this obstacle by himself. This training was augmented by getting the boys to clamber over the rigging of the *Prince Louis*, and up and down nets hung from the dock, which at low tide is exposed high above water. The ropes course became one of the features built into every Outward Bound school. Of course it had to be adapted, particularly in places where no conveniently large trees grew from which to suspend the various ropes and logs. And sometimes it was enlarged upon: several of the American schools have a "high" ropes course—meaning five storeys up in giant conifers and down the sides of considerable precipices.

What would later be called small-group interaction was practised at Aberdovey under the simpler name of co-operation. A dozen boys were mustered into a "watch." which remained together for the entire month and usually established a strong sense of comradeship. Elected positions of captain, quartermaster, bo'sun and others in each watch gave everyone experience in taking responsibility and making critical decisions.

At Aberdovey, too, the lesson of the Good Samaritan was not forgotten. On land and on sea the boys pioneered the rescue work that was to become so much a part of Outward Bound.

The boys kept a record of their own progress in athletics, seamanship and land expeditions, and were put on their honour not to cheat. Watches competed for the prestige of seeing their pennant hoisted on the flagpole. Badges could be earned for individual tasks and upon successful completion of the course.

Taken altogether, the program created an atmosphere that brought forth some of the qualities Lawrence Holt thought were lacking in his young seamen. The training the boys received at Aberdovey toughened their bodies and armed them against the "enemies within"—fear, defeatism, apathy, selfishness.

In 1943 a real survivor of a torpedoing joined the staff of the school. He was Freddie Fuller, a young second mate seconded from the Blue Funnel Line. Twice torpedoed, he had on one occasion commanded a lifeboat for thirty-five days before being rescued. Fuller was actually a reluctant recruit and arrived in an angry mood, fearful that this interruption in sea duty might jeopardize his career. But once again the magic woven by Hahn and those around him worked its wonders. Freddie Fuller was captivated by Hahn's exhortation to his instructors to "fill the lads' cup to overflowing," by the enthusiasm with which Dr. Zimmermann encouraged them in his heavily accented English and made them believe in themselves, and by the school's joyful spirit which renewed itself with every new batch of boys. Although he went back to sea long enough to advance in rank to captain, Fuller threw in his lot with Outward Bound permanently and, when Jim Hogan left, became the second warden of Aberdovey. Now retired and living nearby, Captain Fuller is often visited by "old boys" and always asks them what they remember about those far-off days. "You asked us to do our utmost but never too much," is one frequent answer. And invariably someone will say, "Nothing that I did during the war left as strong an impression on me as those twenty-eight days at Aberdovey."

The name Outward Bound had crept in quietly, and Lawrence Holt is credited with using it first. Outward bound from safe harbour, and homeward bound from a journey, are old seamen's terms. Outward Bound fitted the nature of the training offered at Aberdovey very well indeed. The youngsters embarked in every way upon adventure, into largely uncharted waters, away from the comforts of home and familiar surroundings. The Outward Bound Badge became as coveted as the Gordonstoun, Moray and County badges.

Once the wartime need to train and toughen young sailors

Lawrence Holt *(far right)*, who introduced the name Outward Bound to Aberdovey Sea School

(Capt. F. Fuller)

In the early 'fifties, two watches leaving Aberdovey inner harbour

(Capt. F. Fuller)

had passed, peacetime application of the program seemed logical. Captain Fuller remembers sitting on the javelin field with Lawrence Holt and one or two others and discussing this question. "We asked each other, 'What shall we do when the war is over?' and agreed that Outward Bound was based on sound principles and that with certain modifications it could be made to work as well for other young men as it had for our sailors. We thought that we could find young people in considerable numbers in service clubs, schools, the uniformed services and in industry."

In particular, they looked at industrial apprentices. The apprentice system, a tradition going back to the thirteenth century, continued to be the method by which innumerable lads received their training. Here was a ready pool of young men who could benefit greatly from a month at Outward Bound. Since they would remain with their firms for several years in a situation of mutual loyalty, any experience that would make them healthier, more alert and therefore more productive would be as welcome to the sponsoring employers as to the participants. The logic proved irresistible and apprentices became the backbone of the British Outward Bound schools. Other recruits came from the armed forces, the police and the fire service. Within a few years the training of these young men invariably included a month at Outward Bound.

Aberdovey obviously could not accommodate all of these people. As soon as Gordonstoun School was able to return to Scotland, Hahn pushed to open a second Outward Bound school on his beloved Moray coast. The first warden of the Moray Outward Bound School, Martin Leslie, recalls the financial beginnings of the school in 1948. Hahn had just under £2,000 available to him through the King George V Foundation. He wrote the exact sum, £1,898.18s.9d, on a slip of paper which he handed to Leslie, saying, "Right, Leslie, go away and make a sea school." Once again he had read correctly what manner of man he had chosen for his project. The Moray school was the first to use a board of directors composed of local people to oversee and advise the staff, an administrative setup that became standard Outward Bound practice.

In 1949 an Outward Bound school was opened at Eskdale in the Lake District, a miniature alpine area with many lakes, steep mountains of just over 3,000 feet and, for England, sparse population. Outward Bound was able to acquire one of the gracious homes that dot Britain: a turreted mansion in beautiful grounds complete with a small tarn and surrounded by some of the best rock climbing country in England.

Rock scrambling and hill walking were already part of the program at Aberdovey and Moray. At Eskdale, the whole program was built around mountaineering. This of course required a totally different type of instructor, and for years it was much debated whether they should be avid mountaineers who wished to lead their charges up the most exciting pitches available, or men who used climbing as a means to an end rather than an end in itself. The sea schools had always stressed that the ocean was the medium through which boys learned a lot more than seamanship. At Eskdale, William Blake's statement "Great things happen when men and mountains meet" was taken at face value.

The first warden of Eskdale was Adam Arnold-Brown, an ex-Gordonstoun student who preserved Aberdovey's traditions as much as possible. In this he did not always succeed, partly because of the difference in temperament between seamen who are used to naval discipline and mountaineers to whom self-discipline is more important. One point of contention, for instance, was athletic training: the mountaineering instructors objected to this tradition because they thought the boys were getting plenty of exercise on their climbing expeditions. Arnold-Brown continued to forbid smoking and drinking, though he did allow boys to sign a form stating that they would refrain, instead of having them make this promise in a public ceremony. Of course, this did not always work. When the famous mountaineer Eric Shipton visited Eskdale with a view to taking over the wardenship, he found "a cloud hanging over the school because one boy had been caught smoking; it was as if murder had been done."

Smoking has always been a vexing issue at Outward Bound. Some of those associated with the schools have viewed it as a social evil; others have opposed it because it gets in the way of physical fitness; still others argue that it is not their place to forbid something that is a way of life for many people. And though the ban on smoking means nothing at all to the nonsmokers, it imposes considerable hardship on confirmed smokers, often meaning that they start the Outward Bound course with a distinct handicap.

From its inception, Eskdale has exerted a strong influence on other Outward Bound schools, especially those situated in mountain regions, because of the number of its staff members who have later travelled and become instructors and wardens (or directors) of schools all over the world.

In the postwar years, three more Outward Bound schools were opened: one at Ullswater, which is also in the Lake District; one at Holne Park in Devon, and Rhowniar, an all-girls school a few miles from Aberdovey. The British Army developed an Outward Bound program of its own with centres in Wales and Norway.

Although the great outdoors continued to be Outward Bound's big drawing card, the innovative spirit which Kurt Hahn had implanted in his disciples led to yet another development: City Challenge. This was Captain Fuller's brainchild. "Let's take the lid off cities," Fuller urged when he helped start the program in 1967, "and send our students to that part which is known only to the police, social workers, hospital attendants and the Salvation Army." He insisted that wilderness was to be found not only in mountains and upon the sea but also in homes for the aged, among physically and mentally handicapped people, immigrants, delinquents, the destitute and the homeless. Cities were a wilderness in which challenges could be found for young people. All the usual segments of the Outward Bound Standard Course could be transferred to the crowded streets and back alleys of Britain's large, grimy industrial cities. Sea and mountain rescue techniques could be translated to the rescue of the flotsam and jetsam in urban centres.

Young people may live in cities all their lives without ever meeting the soft urban underbelly; when they do, it can be as alarming as the first step of a rappel down a cliff. And not only for students. The typical Outward Bound instructor, well versed in outdoor education, often faded in the face of this kind of wilderness and had to be replaced by someone with a background in social and youth services. Yet City Challenge was typically Outward Bound. As in the early days of Aberdovey, students ventured into the unknown, and had to improvise. Before games and sports could be taught to underprivileged city children, for instance, facilities had to be built in empty lots and odd halls, officials had to be persuaded, suspicions overcome. A course had to be devised among the man-made cliffs and cheerless hospital corridors that would do for students what the fickle tides of Cardigan Bay and the sombre Welsh hills had done for their predecessors.

In his last years at Aberdovey, Captain Fuller used to send some of the boys to work for a day at Aberystwith Hospital. "They used to come back quite shattered," he recalls. "I suppose our young people were pretty sheltered from the sadness and horror of terminal illness, the bloody results of accidents, and death. The sentiment of compassion was not a popular one but we made sure it had a place in Outward Bound."

In 1946 the Outward Bound Trust was established as an umbrella organization for the British schools to look after fund raising, publicity and recruitment of staff and students. It also serves as the body that can give new schools in other countries permission, in the form of a charter, to operate under the name Outward Bound. The charter is given to a national organization such as Outward Bound Inc. in the United States, The Outward Bound Trust of Hong Kong, or Deutsche Gesellschaft für Europäische Erziehung in West Germany, and these organizations are then responsible for any schools in their country.

Dr. Bernhard Zimmermann inspired the boys with his enthusiasm for sport.
(Capt. F. Fuller)

A charter is only granted when the British Trust is satisfied that the newly created school is prepared to accept the basic principles of Outward Bound and will run courses generally in line with those in Britain and others already operating. This protective device became particularly important when Outward Bound was copied in various ways with, and sometimes without, permission from the parent body (see chapter 8).

Outward Bound Associations in many cities throughout Britain keep the fires of Outward Bound burning brightly. Composed of alumni, sponsors and interested people generally, the associations are active in publicizing the schools and raising money to sponsor students.

After nearly forty years of Outward Bound, which in the beginning was a response to a desperate wartime need, it has unquestionably made a secure place for itself in Britain, and its name has become a household word.

Chapter 4
The Peak Is a Point
in the Journey

It was a joy for Kurt Hahn to observe towards the end of his life how the ideas he had formulated so long ago had travelled over the years and across the miles of ocean and land. The first Outward Bound schools beyond the United Kingdom were in the British Commonwealth. The British model was at first copied faithfully, but soon each school made changes in order to become more in tune with local geographical and social conditions.

AFRICA

Outward Bound schools started in the vast African continent on a note of tremendous enthusiasm, which could not be sustained once the British Empire was dismantled. In the birth pangs of independence African schools have had a rough time and some have gone under. The latest political upheavals have created severe problems, not the least of which is the disruption of postal services so that it is often virtually impossible for outsiders to obtain up-to-date information.

In 1956 an Outward Bound school was started at **Loitokitok** in **Kenya,** partway up the north slope of Mount Kilimanjaro. The most encouraging feature of this school was the deliberate mixing of students of widely differing backgrounds. The three races who share the country—European, African and East Indian—each arrived at Outward Bound with their own strengths, weaknesses and prejudices. Peter Ryce was on one of the first courses there as a schoolboy and remembers it vividly: "We all excelled at different things. The Africans were sensational runners. We obtained our drinking water from a well two miles away and all had to take turns getting it. The Kenyan boys were always back with their full buckets while the rest of us still plodded towards the well. The Europeans automatically assumed a leadership role in the patrol. The Asians were self-effacing and gave up easily when the going got rough. We all had to make adjustments. We also had to contend with strong tribal taboos within the African groups."

Mount Kilimanjaro is a 19,300-foot mountain of volcanic origin straddling the border between Kenya and what used to be German East Africa, then Tanganyika and is now Tanzania. Standard Courses included an ascent of one of the twin peaks, and for students from the coastal regions this meant moving through an incredible vertical cross section of the country. Peter Ryce again: "You start at the steamy and hot seashore. At 2,000 to 3,000 feet there is arid semi-desert, followed by lush rain forest. Between 9,000 and 15,000 feet you walk through tufted grass and giant heathers, ferns and nettles. Beyond that the rock is bare and crowned by a permanent icefield. It is not unusual to wake up above the 16,000-foot level to find one's bivouac covered by snow and the temperature below freezing. All this on the equator of course."

The school staff made great efforts to adapt the program to

the particular problems of Kenya while it was engaged in the painful transition from colony to sovereign state. Mike Perry worked at Loitokitok in the early 1960s and visited the school again ten years later: "We had to moderate the Christian ethic and tailor morning devotions to be relevant to our Moslem, Hindu and pagan students. Before independence [in 1973], Outward Bound was one of the few places in Kenya where the different races could get to know each other and where fixed attitudes could be modified. Black, white and brown skinned boys were profoundly influenced by the mere fact of being in a patrol where each took his turn leading, sweeping floors, deciding where to camp and fetching water. The newly independent state sent many aspiring police, forestry, civil service and military trainees to Outward Bound. These are the people who are now running the country and who have been shaped in part by what they learned there."

Unfortunately, in the 1970s political clashes with Uganda and Tanzania proliferated; special permission to climb Mount Kilimanjaro had to be obtained; enrolment, money and other support decreased sharply, and equipment deteriorated. The latest news from Loitokitok is that plans are being made to move the school around the mountain so that it will be well within Kenyan borders.

An ascent of Mount Kilimanjaro is also the high point of the twenty-six-day Standard Course at the **Tanzania Outward Bound School**. The program follows the British model closely: two weeks at the school headquarters, two weeks divided among short expeditions. The three-day training expedition and two-day Solo are done on the flanks of the mountain at altitudes between 9,000 and 12,000 feet. Then there is a four-day plains expedition in the jungle and a final expedition to the peak of Kilimanjaro. Most of the courses are for boys and young men; schoolgirls and working girls attend their own programs, and coed programs are going to be introduced shortly.

In 1965 a school was opened at **Mbala**, in **Zambia**. Courses are held in jungle and hilly areas, but most of the activities are centred on a lake. The majority of students are trainees from the copper industry.

Lesotho (the former Basutoland), while totally surrounded by South Africa, has retained enough independence to be able to ignore apartheid. In 1974 an Outward Bound school was established at **Thaba Phatsoa** in northwestern Lesotho. Buildings were specially designed and built by local labour with funds largely provided by the Anglo-American Corporation and other mining companies. The land was donated by the state with the consent of the local chiefs. Built at the 5,400-foot level in mountains reaching over 10,000 feet, Thaba Phatsoa is essentially a mountain school, but a few rivers and a lake make canoeing and sailing possible as well.

Bob Jickling, who was an instructor there recently, describes it as "a small school which can take about fifty students at any one time. The country is great for expeditions, having lots of good climbing. The 'great abseil'—200 feet high—must be one of the longest rappels anywhere. Most of the students work for the mining companies and are sponsored by them. Few come at their own expense or from outside Lesotho except for one or two whose homes are in Soweto or Swaziland. No doubt the fact that the school is multiracial is the greatest challenge to both students and staff."

Melsetter in **Zimbabwe** (the former Rhodesia), established in 1961 close to the border with Mozambique, was another Outward Bound school that had a good record of black and white students working together peaceably. For years it struggled to keep going in spite of sanctions imposed on Rhodesia, Portuguese-led terrorist groups raiding across the border and the generally embattled state of the country. By 1979, however, Melsetter had become a police training camp.

ASIA

After World War II, the Far East did not see real peace for many years. A long period of guerilla warfare preceded **Malaysia**'s emergence as an independent nation, which started to

Outward Bound in Malaysia: uninhabited islands, coral reefs, and an occasional shark to keep the watch alert
(photograph by Ray Preece)

build a society where Malays, Chinese, Indians and Europeans could work together. Outward Bound made its contribution by opening a school in 1954, and in the best spirit of this multiracial society the first school director was British, the second Chinese, the third and present director Indian. Until 1977 the school was situated within a military compound on the west coast of Malaysia, south of Penang; now it has been moved to an isolated bay nearby. The coastal scenery is beautiful: a variety of uninhabited islands with sandy beaches invite shore camping and the coral reefs tempt divers; an occasional shark cruises around to keep everyone alert. Students are sent to Outward Bound mostly by large commercial companies and by the military. They go on jungle expeditions and learn seamanship in kayaks, whalers and a ketch. A second school will soon be opened on the east coast of Malaysia.

At the tip of the Malay Peninsula lies **Singapore**, the great sprawling city that was once a jewel of the British Imperial Crown and is now an independent city-state. It has hardly anything that could be called a hinterland and no natural resources. Its wealth lies in its people, half of whom are under twenty-one years old. Beginning in 1960, the British Army conducted an Adventure School for young people. Out of this grew an Outward Bound School on the island of **Pulau Ubin** not far from the city. Its chief aims are to harness the "youth power" of Singapore and to further peaceful coexistence between the Chinese, Malay and Indian citizens. This school always was and continues to be run by the military; its city office is in the Ministry of Defence compound, and the students come almost exclusively from the uniformed services.

The colony of **Hong Kong** is luckier than Singapore in that it does have a hinterland—the New Territories. Outside the teeming city of Kowloon there are innumerable bays and inlets, sawtooth mountain crags and deep valleys. Outward Bound was able to have a school near Sai Kung until a national park was created in the area and thousands of visitors began flocking there on weekends and holidays. Warden Jack Tucker is now busy raising money to build a brigantine large enough to house forty-three students and nine officers. He hopes that by 1981 the Hong Kong Outward Bound course will take place entirely on the China Seas aboard a splendid new ship.

DOWN UNDER

In 1959 **Outward Bound Australia** was opened at Fisherman's Point on the Hawkesbury River in New South Wales. It had several things in common with the British schools, including base camp in an existing large mansion (Carter House), athletic training, a tight timetable, carefully defined duties, flag raising and inspection of quarters. Geographically, of course, it differed enormously. Carter House was built on an isolated strip of shoreline accessible only by boat. In fact, canoes, surf-boats, a whaler and assorted other craft provided a fair-sized armada in which the students could learn seamanship. A 100-mile-long inland expedition route combined travel by river and on foot through almost uninhabited countryside. Patrols would leave base camp in opposite directions and link up for a short spell approximately halfway.

Fisherman's Point had to be closed in 1973 partly for financial reasons and partly because of the remoteness of the school which made movement of people and supplies difficult. It was reopened at **Tharwa**, closer to Sydney, under the leadership of Garry Richards, an Australian educator who gave the school an entirely different direction and emphasis. He expanded the program to include "Pack and Paddle" courses for younger children and four-day programs for sponsors. Girls were made welcome though not many came. (Richards has a problem there: coed courses would have an average of only 1.7 women in each group of students. The proportions are better balanced on courses for men and women over thirty years.)

Bushwalking, caving, "cascading" (paddling an inflated air mattress downriver), life-rafting on rivers and in the ocean,

Australia has adopted the American-pioneered "mobile" course in Victoria and in Queensland; students spend the entire course out-of-doors.
(Outward Bound Australia)

hiking through tropical rain forests and visiting islands on the Great Barrier Reef provide a uniquely "Aussie" flavour to the school. The Australians have also adopted the American-pioneered "mobile" courses which allow students to spend the entire course out-of-doors without ever returning to base camp. These journeys are undertaken in Victoria in the south and in Queensland in the north.

Service to the community is an important part of the school's program. In the south this consists of helping local property owners with fencing and clearing fields, as well as cleaning cave sites and bushwalking huts. In North Queensland students live the best part of a week on ships chartered to take them to the Great Barrier Reef islands and they contribute to the running and maintenance of the craft—steering, standing watches, scrubbing decks, painting.

The Australian school puts great value on the inspirational readings that have largely replaced the morning prayers traditional in the British and British-inspired schools. Garry Richards writes: "We control the psychological environment very seriously and consequently have established a number of set readings at set times during the course. These are given by only a limited number of people who practise hard at getting the right effect so that the readings become meaningful and are not left to chance. I think our readings are of great value—the style tends to be brief, undramatic but effective."

A teacher himself, Richards is inclined to pick his instructors from the teaching profession, though over the years there have been engineers, dentists and a senior detective. Staff go through various training exercises and earn qualifications that carry extra pay.

Outward Bound South Australia has had a somewhat chequered history. In 1961 a group of Adelaide businessmen and retired seamen started the Arkaba Adventure School in the Flinders Range of South Australia. It ran into troubles similar to those at Fisherman's Point—financial shortages and problems with moving people and supplies to the isolated site. In

1967 land was acquired at **Clayton**, close to Lake Alexandria on the Murray River, where a sea school was opened to take advantage of ocean, lake and river. The name was changed to Outward Bound South Australia and a charter obtained from the Australian Trust in Sydney. The climate at Clayton is dry: fresh water is chronically short; when it rains, the whole program is scrapped and everyone goes whitewater canoeing. This school runs Standard Courses for only three months of the year; the rest of the time is given over to contract courses for students from private schools, police cadets and people sent by businesses and banks.

Cobham Outward Bound School at Anakiwa, **New Zealand**, was started in 1962 with the enormous advantage of a $200,000 endowment that had been raised before it ever opened its doors. Base camp is a hotel near Picton, a resort town on the south side of Cook Strait which lies between the North and South islands. One enchanted visitor wrote: "I found this to be a mixture of Norway, Austria, the Riviera and a South Sea island. Expeditions sail to lonely islands, canoe down romantic rivers and climb in magnificent mountains." Although only a few women take courses and coed courses are nonexistent, the New Zealand program expects everyone, girls and boys, to perform considerable physical feats, stressing challenge as its main object. That same visitor observed with awe: "A girls' group was canoeing down a river having three- and four-degree rapids. At one point the instructor told the girls to jump out of their boats, tow them ashore, climb a vertical cliff and dive back into the river."

The school is in an area largely controlled by parks boards, and in return for unlimited use of these lands, students help with track clearing, cleaning and maintaining camp and picnic sites. Another service project is supervising mentally handicapped children who come to the school for a week's holiday.

Cobham has a novel way of keeping confidential the identity of delinquent youngsters who are sent to them by the authorities. Head office makes all the bookings and places information

Somewhere below, a kayak
(Outward Bound New Zealand)

regarding such people in a separate, sealed envelope which is only opened in the case of a "reluctant student," as former director John Mitchell delicately expressed it. However, he added, "usually the troublesome person is not the one in the envelope." Unusual, too, is the school's method of dealing with situations that require someone to take charge: "We don't appoint or elect formal leaders but expect individuals with particular skills to take on this role for the duration of the situation that requires solving. Leadership is thus changed as the group moves from problem to problem."

As is the case at Outward Bound Australia, Cobham also considers some form of inspirational readings important. A daily morning parade concludes with a reading from an author whose lifestyle or thinking reflects on some value the school thinks worth promoting. John Mitchell used readings from many sources—from explorers such as Scott, Shackleton, Hillary, Sir John Hunt, Saint-Exupéry, Drake, Nelson and their own founder and patron, Lord Cobham; from authors like H.G. Wells, Robert Louis Stevenson, Morris West; as well as from Kurt Hahn. "At full musters I usually read these," Mitchell says, "but at smaller ones (one or two watches) instructors may do so. These are very valuable. Instructors' briefings to students going on Solo are also always accompanied by appropriate readings." All parades conclude with a final prayer, and all meals begin with grace offered by students, or with a period of silence.

The New Zealand Outward Bound school has earned a high reputation. With some employers, an Outward Bound course has become a mandatory part of their training program. They may also send trainees as a reward for productivity, or else as a last resort: "If you can't sort him out, he's sacked." Service clubs send young people to Outward Bound for a variety of reasons: to the high achiever, such as a Queen's Scout, Head Pupil or Duke of Edinburgh Award winner, it's a reward; for a lad in trouble with the police, it's rehabilitation; but dozens are selected by lot, leaving it all to chance.

EUROPE

Almost a decade after the end of World War II, the first Outward Bound school was opened in **West Germany**, which pleased Kurt Hahn immensely. This was a sea school on the North Sea (since closed), and it was followed in 1956 by a mountain school at **Baad** and in 1969 by another at **Berchtesgaden**. Termed *Kurzschulen*—short-term schools—they had to evolve in an atmosphere totally different from that of the British and British-inspired schools. Anything smacking of militarism was anathema to a large segment of the German postwar population. This distaste was felt so strongly that new names had to be found for such innocent places as equipment stores, which could not be called *Bekleidungskammer* because the word had been used by the army. The German schools also differ from the British and North American models in their funding: thirty-three per cent of their income comes from the federal government. As one of the school directors explains, "It means that we have to be constantly at pains to legitimize our activities in their eyes, to be worthy of their generosity."

In the make-up of their student body the *Kurzschulen* are closer to the British than to the North American schools. The boys and girls who come to them are definitely the "average" young Germans rather than youngsters who are already motivated to try something as unusual and adventurous as Outward Bound. The two school directors don't mind; on the contrary, they feel that their programs have been designed specifically for such young people.

Kurzschule students are housed in large, Bavarian-style buildings in magnificent surroundings. They sleep in comfortable four-bed rooms, and are issued first-class skiing, climbing and canoeing equipment. The food in Baad is the tastiest I have eaten in all the schools I visited.

Although the rock climbing and high mountain touring are as challenging as any, "roughing it" is not part of the program. Outward Bound tradition has had to be reconciled with Alpine tradition, foremost in which is the unwritten rule that climbers must be led by qualified guides. This makes unaccompanied expeditions impossible and does not permit any kind of Solo. As everywhere in the Alps, the tourist dollar is king: with one or two exceptions, there is no camping out, and students cannot even cook their own meals on expeditions but must use staffed mountain huts. Their canoes and inflatable rafts are chased away from rivers and lakes by local innkeepers who have boats for rent and object to private craft.

Both schools are right on the Austrian-German border, which can cause all kinds of problems. For example, the one exception to the no camping rule is Berchtesgaden's canoe camp, pitched in a pleasant valley bottom on both sides of a small creek that actually is the frontier. The sleeping tents and campfire square are on the more suitable flat area on the Austrian side, but the kitchen and supply tent is on the German side since otherwise an extra tax would have to be paid for the provisions. All food is therefore cooked and stored in Germany, carried across a couple of planks laid over the creek and eaten in Austria.

Outward Bound traditionalists cringe at the sight of students smoking while waiting to climb the next rock pitch, or downing a pint of beer in the small pubs called *Kellerbars* run by both schools on their premises. "And why not," counter school directors Ulf Händel of Baad and Rolf Mantler of Berchtesgaden. "In the short period available to us we cannot make nonsmokers out of smokers, though we do stress the potential dangers of cigarettes. And since both schools are in the middle of tourist centres and surrounded by restaurants all serving beer, we think it more sensible to offer the students the same thing 'at home' where they can drink more cheaply and under our supervision. Besides, Bavarians imbibe beer with their mothers' milk and who are we to try to forbid it? By the same token we don't bother too much about messy rooms; teaching them to be tidy is their parents' job, not ours."

The educational basis upon which Outward Bound was origi-

In the German mountain schools, the word "hiking" does not apply.
(Kurzschule Baad)

At Baad, mountain rescues are practised in training sessions as well as in real emergencies.

(Kurzschule Baad)

Avalanche rescue: a line of *Kurzschule* students probe for buried victims.

(Kurzschule Baad)

nally built is taken very seriously. The word "paedagogical" appears frequently in *Kurzschule* literature: "students who come to us must be paedagogically motivated." Instructors all have a background in teaching, either in the social sciences—*Sozialpaedagogen*—or in physical education—*Sportpaedagogen*. The latter must either possess mountain guiding certificates or acquire them within two years of joining the *Kurzschule* staff.

"Political education" is included in the educational aims, and at first glance that seems vaguely suspect, especially coming from Germany. However, this is politics in the sense of Plato's concept of *polis*—the city as a democratic institution. "Political education" is thus actually social education, closer in orientation to the leadership training, citizenship and self-help schemes at African and Asian schools than to politics in the accepted sense. And just as schools in the former British colonies emphasize giving members of different racial groups an opportunity to meet, so in the thoroughly stratified German society, the *Kurzschulen* provide a common meeting ground for high school and university students, industrial apprentices and other disparate types who would otherwise seldom meet.

As do other schools around the world, the two German ones have taken on the "colouring" of their respective directors. Ulf Händel of Baad is a compact mountain man whose deeply lined face could have come out of a wood carving. He runs his school on highly structured lines: elected student leaders take over some of the administrative chores; a card index with students' photos and particulars in the staff common room allows for easy identification; a loudspeaker summons everyone to meals and activities. Meticulously detailed time schedules list evening activities such as folk dancing, crafts, movies, botany and geology lectures as well as free time.

But Baad is above all a mountain school. Apart from spending some time river rafting and on an easy ropes and obstacle course, students move high up among the peaks where the word hiking does not apply. It is all honest-to-goodness mountaineering and, in winter, tough skiing. The Good Samaritan is

A contrast in school facilities: the gracious mansion of Zee en Bergscholen
Nederland

(Outward Bound Holland)

. . . and the typical Bavarian resort hotel of Baad

(Kurzschule Baad)

very active here: the school's mountain rescue log is crammed with entries.

There is quite a different atmosphere at Berchtesgaden. Rolf Mantler tackles his job with unbounded enthusiasm, a great deal of voluble theorizing and a light hand on the reins of administration. He is a beanpole of a man in his early thirties who does not believe in elected or appointed group leaders and is constantly trying to make his courses as exciting as possible in the manicured Alps. A canoe camp, a cave behind a frozen waterfall where winter students may spend a night, and a small hut where students can do their own cooking are a beginning in that direction, but one of his ambitions is to provide real mobile courses and at least some form of Solo.

The *Kurzschulen* have been described as more inward than outward bound, and there is some truth in that. Although students are expected to extend themselves physically, a real spirit of adventure is noticeably absent, especially compared to many other schools. Every square inch of the mountains and valleys has been trod countless times, every step the students take is carefully supervised by the guides, and nothing is left to chance. The justifications cited are the great difficulty of the mountain terrain and the unpredictable weather. Another kind of challenge therefore has to be substituted. This takes the form of group dynamics, constructive criticism and self-criticism, and much discussion of what to do, when to do it and how to do it—all, however, within well-defined limits.

In **Holland**, Outward Bound was started in 1961 on a small island off the Dutch coast. It offers a twenty-two-day Standard Course for fifteen- to twenty-three-year-olds, and a twelve-day course for people up to forty. Rock climbing is done in the Ardennes.

Harald Becker, a young German instructor whom I met at Baad, worked for a while in the Dutch school and found it enjoyable but demanding: "I had to learn a lot in a very short time. For instance, I discovered that my experience of paddling a canoe on a mountain river in the Alps did not prepare me for

Mountaineering without mountains
(Outward Bound Holland)

canoeing on the busy waterways of Holland. It was unnerving! I thought I knew how to judge the speed and manoeuvrability of a canoe, but confronted by large freighters bearing down on my tiny craft, I had to think and act quite differently."

The program at this school is prescribed for the first three or four days, but after that it is up to the students and staff to work out what they want to do and when. This can lead to interesting situations, as Harald Becker recalls: "One day, about halfway through an expedition, we instructors announced we wanted a day off and would remain in our tent. The students went into a huddle and had some heated discussion. Then they made their decision. They simply pulled the tent down over our heads and told us that since everyone had agreed on the details of this trip, everyone would also carry it out. It was very good for them to come to this conclusion and for us to know that we could be overruled."

An Outward Bound program was started in **Belgium** in 1977 under the leadership of L.M. Lefebvre, professor of sports psychology at the Catholic University of Leuven (Louvain). This is very much a short-term school—courses for young people last about a week and those for executives two or three days. However, students may come back several times since the program varies from year to year. The courses are coed except those offered to high school girls.

Professor Lefebvre says that the school is a joint venture of university and business and is supported by government funds. "The approach is a scientific one, using carefully supervised and measured methods of Action and Reflection, with much verbal and nonverbal communication between the participants and instructors. Everyone is encouraged to reflect upon their experience and use these conclusions constructively." Rock climbing, for instance, is not just a matter of getting up and down a rock face but also includes the compiling of data to see exactly what happens to students who engage in this activity. Studies of various kinds are carried out to investigate how Outward Bound affects physical education teachers in the areas of co-operation, motivation, leadership style and self-assurance, and how executives gain in teamwork and interpersonal trust. Since 1979 special courses for the blind have been held.

Looking at Outward Bound around the world it is obvious that each warden and school director has felt free to shape his or her school according to a personal vision, the capacities of the staff and the opportunities offered by the particular country. It is almost as if all these people had attended the memorial service held for Kurt Hahn at Gordonstoun at which Henry Brereton, his successor there, made a memorable speech. He told the boys that he wanted them to be sure they would not thoughtlessly throw out traditions which had become outmoded, without replacing them with something equally worthwhile and, in the new context, relevant: "Certainly submit these traditions to searching investigation as Kurt Hahn did, as those who followed him were forever doing, to be sure that they have not become meaningless or treated with slovenly disrespect. For the new form must be as vivid, as memorable, as was the old at its best, and never devoid of the same fundamental meaning as the old embodied."

Chapter 5
Outward Bound
Crosses the Atlantic

When the seeds of Outward Bound were carried across the Atlantic and rooted in the vast continent of North America, they grew into a rather different plant. True, the basic concepts that had been so successful in Britain were all there, but from the beginning the American and Canadian schools considered themselves much freer than any of the others to improvise, adapt and modify. They had to, given the geographical range, and the totally different backgrounds from which their students came.

Virtually nothing that worked in Britain could be copied without a good hard look. No aspect of the Outward Bound course could be used merely because it was tradition, for traditions had often grown out of simple expedient. The original Standard Course, for example, was twenty-eight days long rather than twenty-five or twenty-nine because this covered exactly two pay periods for the British apprentices. The North American schools soon found themselves developing their own "traditions" to suit their own environments. The size of brigades at the Minnesota school is a good example: it was set at eight plus two instructors only because no more than ten people are allowed in the campsites of the Boundary Waters Canoe Area through which they frequently travel. At the Hurricane Island sea school, the watch equals the number of students, plus two watch officers, plus everybody's equipment that will fit into one of the school's specially designed boats.

From 1962 on, seven Outward Bound schools were opened in the United States and two in Canada. No two schools were ever the same but they were all unmistakably Outward Bound. This is not so astonishing when one considers that, with the exception of Hurricane Island, the North American schools were begun and at first staffed by people who had already received generous doses of "The Hahn Prescription" and had been infected with Kurt Hahn's enthusiasm for new ventures.

There were, for instance, the three men primarily responsible for bringing Outward Bound to the United States—Joshua Miner III, Joe Nold and Capt. Freddie Fuller.

Josh Miner, a young American teacher with a degree from Princeton, went to teach at Gordonstoun in the early 1950s. By the time he left the school, he had resolved to spend the rest of his life carrying out the educational and humanitarian goals of Kurt Hahn. "No one," he says, "could have a meal with Hahn every day for two years as I did without being profoundly influenced by him." When he first returned to the United States, however, he was not sure whether to promote another Gordonstoun, a United World College or an Outward Bound school. Then a number of things happened to help him make up his mind. The launching of the Soviet's Sputnik revealed how badly the United States was lagging in the space race; educational practices were first questioned and then radically overhauled as a result. President Kennedy's famous inaugural speech "Ask not what your country can do for you but what you can do for your country" ushered in a spirit of service that led to the creation of the Peace Corps, Vista and other programs in which young Americans could help their fellow men. By 1962 Miner considered the time was ripe for Outward Bound and set about raising $1 million to get it started.

Joe Nold, a young Canadian, had also worked at Gordonstoun. Although he had a law degree, he never practised and instead divided his time between his great love, mountaineering, and his great interest, teaching. When the idea for an American Outward Bound school was talked about, his eyes naturally turned towards the mountains for a suitable site.

Capt. Freddie Fuller, who had taken over the position of warden at Aberdovey in 1945, was sent to the United States by the Outward Bound Trust to act as a special consultant with these two enthusiasts. The three of them inspected several possible school sites and all agreed that one in Colorado appeared to be the best. Fuller also spoke to groups of potential supporters all over the country, introducing Americans to Outward Bound. Before returning to England, he flew to Puerto Rico at the request of the administrators of the Peace Corps organization to assist in choosing a site and setting up a training program after the Outward Bound pattern. The next year he returned there to supervise the first courses.

The **Colorado Outward Bound School** started in 1962 with a few summer courses. The British Outward Bound Trust gave it their blessing, first with formal permission for a pilot project, and eventually with the granting of an Outward Bound charter. Joe Nold became school director—a title that seemed more appropriate than the British term, warden.

Innovation and experimentation became everyday activities at the Colorado school. Joe Nold kept careful note of what seemed to make each course successful. For instance, many students told him that they had particularly enjoyed the short period of solitude called the Solo but wished it had been longer than a night and part of a day. The three-day, three-night Solo to which it was lengthened became the standard Solo in all

Outward Bound schools subsequently opened in the country.

Nold and his staff also noticed that the students found living in buildings less attractive than living in tents, and sleeping under the stars even more to their liking. They began to experiment with the customary pattern of the British Standard Course which allowed students fourteen days in the school itself and twelve days divided among short expeditions. They sent their students on longer and longer expeditions until eventually most of the courses at Colorado became mobile. Students picked up their gear at a central point and did not return until the end of the course, sleeping out the whole time. Although this was a break with tradition, the mobile courses turned out to be the most powerful attraction of Outward Bound for many North American students. The patrol, brigade or watch—as the small groups were called in the different schools—which stayed together throughout the course, often under trying circumstances, had a splendid chance of becoming a single, well-functioning unit. As each new school was established, it soon found a distinctive way of fitting mobile courses to the terrain—backpacking and ski mountaineering in the mountains, sailing cutters on the coast, paddling fully loaded canoes on lakes and rivers.

As a result of this trend, school buildings became less and less important. Unlike the British schools, most of which are housed in large and imposing mansions, the American schools have placed little importance on structures. Several of them operate out of small offices, storing their equipment in warehouses: most of their courses are mobile ones.

In 1964 a second school was started in Minnesota by Bob Pieh, an American educator who had corresponded for years with Kurt Hahn though the two men had never met. The **Minnesota Outward Bound School**—MOBS for short—lies at the edge of the two million acres of true wilderness that is called the Boundary Waters Canoe Area on the American side of the border and Quetico Provincial Park in Canada. On a map this huge area is a watery maze of lakes and streams held together by thin strips of land. Here motorboats are severely restricted, and tin cans forbidden outright (park rangers have the authority to confiscate them).

In winter everything is hidden under a blanket of deep snow, the rivers imprisoned beneath thick ice, the frozen lakes an expanse of untrodden white ringed by the green-black of brooding forest. Outward Bound students move through the country in magnificent solitude, the swish of skis on crisp snow the only sound.

Summertime fire drill evacuation of base camp—which is called Homeplace—is eerie and unforgettable. The school takes to all available boats and heads into the middle of the lake shrouded in predawn mist. Silence is instinctive and total. The night creatures have gone to sleep and the day ones are not yet awake. Every bit of landscape colour is washed out. Water, shoreline, canoes and their occupants are nothing but a tracing of black, grey and white.

In these surroundings, an offshoot of the mobile course, called the "immersion route," developed. Students arrive by bus in a small clearing, expecting cabins or tents, dining hall and a gradual introduction to Outward Bound. Instead, they are met by instructors who have brought canoes already loaded with food, sleeping bags and other gear; they are told to leave their luggage in the buses and to get into the boats. Off they go for a period of five or more days, plunged straightaway into the simplicity of living in the woods with the minimum of accustomed comforts, constantly on the move either paddling or portaging their canoes, preparing and eating very basic foods and making camp each night in a different spot. As they go along they learn woodcraft, map reading, the safe way to navigate their heavily laden canoes. This must be the quickest and most effective way for people to discover how much they depend on each other, and how much more they are able to do than they ever imagined they could. By the time they finally arrive at base camp, the group of strangers has already begun to function as a cohesive unit.

Brigades that are judged to have been particularly successful at learning to work as a group are granted an extra privilege: an unaccompanied expedition. They work out their exact route, decide how far they can go each day, how much and what food to take. The instructors travel a few hours behind them and look for messages that the brigades must leave twice a day in prearranged places. They never meet, but are not far apart in case something should go wrong.

The immersion route from **Hurricane Island Outward Bound School**, on that airy hump of granite off the coast of Maine, takes the form of two watch officers mustering a dozen students on their arrival at the nearest mainland wharf, issuing them with foul-weather gear, and setting sail. Sometimes the watch never gets to Hurricane Island at all but spends the whole time sailing and only occasionally landing at some out-of-the-way, uninhabited island. Coast guard regulations make it mandatory that one person with a valid operator's certificate be on each boat, so there is no such thing as an unaccompanied expedition for students. Watch officers try to approximate this, however, by pretending to be invisible, and at least one has been quoted as telling her students that even if they were heading straight for the rocks she would not interfere.

The founder and director of Hurricane Island is Peter Willauer, a tall, soft-spoken Princeton graduate, a teacher and life-long sailor. He had set his heart on an island setting for the school, because "islands are special. Those who step on their shores leave everything behind them. Problems as well as possessions remain on the mainland and a definite island mentality quickly surfaces. Nothing is as important as the sea in all its vagaries, the weather, the tides, the sea-worthiness of your ship and the seamanship of yourself and those who sail with you." He found his island, and an almost perfect setting for Outward Bound it proved to be. Wonderfully solid granite cliffs and the perpendicular walls of a disused quarry provide excellent rock climbing. A grove of reasonably sized trees is tailor-made for a good ropes course. Hurricane Island is within easy reach of hundreds of other islands as well as rivers, bays and inlets on the mainland. Abundant marine life and many edible plants make this one of the very few Outward Bound schools in the world where foraging for food on Solo is possible. Storms, fog, tricky tides, a rocky shoreline and other hazards offer enough natural challenges to satisfy the most demanding designer of Outward Bound courses.

Peter Willauer had never set foot in an Outward Bound school before setting up Hurricane Island in 1965—deliberately. He felt that, had he done so, he might have been tempted to copy and not to think the whole operation through for himself. Yet by some strange, almost magical transference of thought and action, he and his staff have carried on the tradition of Aberdovey. At the same time the school has a contemporary American feeling, in which professionalism and idealism are mixed in healthy proportion.

The term "roughing it" takes on a special meaning for students who are introduced to one of the dozen boats specially designed for Hurricane Island. Officially they are described as thirty-foot-long, six-foot-wide, double-ended, open, ketch-rigged pulling boats; to the landlubbers they look like big row-boats with two masts and two square sails. The operative word is "open"— there is no shelter except what can be rigged with plastic sheets; gear and personal belongings are stored under the thwarts. At night, sleeping bags are spread on top of oars laid across the width of the boat. One girl told me, "Heaven was drawing the flat rather than the round end of the oars."

Since watch officers and students are together in such cramped and often very uncomfortable quarters, the composition of each watch has to be carefully engineered to minimize possible points of friction. It is rather like playing Russian roulette with the weather, the peculiarities of the students and the personalities of the watch officers. These ingredients can make or break an expedition—and only the last variable is known. The trick is to second-guess how each watch will react to good and to bad weather. It is nice if the weather is fine, but

Two of Hurricane Island's pulling boats homeward bound
(Hurricane Island Outward Bound School)

it can be too fine, so that students don't have to pit themselves against the elements. "It would be ideal if one could only summon up a storm and then, when the students are at their wits' end with the cold, wet, navigation problems, seasickness, too much rowing, too little sailing and general misery, bring out the sun and calm the sea!" says Peter Willauer with considerable feeling. This is an echo of Kurt Hahn's standing orders to his teachers: "Dunk them and then dry them out."

The quantity and quality of the food a watch takes on expeditions is a critical part of the gamble. Food can become a point of contention in any community, but in the choppy waters off Maine, stomachs are often queasy and seasickness always around the corner even on calm days. Peter Willauer has long been concerned with this. To get away from the usual institutional kind of meals, he hired Rick Perry, a health food store and restaurant owner, to provide good food that would please most of the people—an almost impossible assignment.

"People identify with food," Perry says. "They are loath to try anything new. Youngsters from the poorest homes have the greatest aversion to trying new foods, so we introduce it to them slowly and gradually."

Rick Perry has practically stopped buying ready-made provisions. In a grain room he grinds all his own flour from a variety of grains. Great bins contain the ingredients for porridge and granola, and legumes of all kinds including the versatile soy bean. He makes tofu (the Japanese soy bean cake which is highly nutritious), yoghurt, miso paste and chickpea paste (humus). Some watches thrive on largely vegetarian rations and eat every scrap; others arrive back at Hurricane Island on the verge of mutiny and dying for hot dogs.

At Hurricane Island it is also possible to fulfil one requirement that was always close to Kurt Hahn's heart—that students in any institution with which he was connected should in some way serve their fellow men. Josh Miner is sure that Hahn would have loved to plant an Outward Bound school six miles out of New York City or in Boston Harbor, "because there would be no shortage of victims to rescue." Hurricane Island does the next best thing: it is part of the U.S. coast guard network and keeps a twenty-four radio watch. Calls for assistance are frequent and promptly answered. However, because so many of the American schools are in isolated settings, this kind of immediate service to the community is not always possible for their students. The search for other ways of fulfilling Hahn's beloved Good Samaritan requirement led to "adaptive programs"—Outward Bound courses for special groups, particularly delinquent youngsters, prison inmates, the mentally and physically handicapped (see chapter 11).

The unlikeliest home for Outward Bound in the United States is among the ivy-covered, mellow brick buildings and tree-shaded paths of Dartmouth College in New Hampshire. The **Dartmouth Outward Bound Center**—it is not called a school in deference to its singular ties with the university—is the first and only result of a vision shared by Josh Miner and Charles Dey of the Tucker Foundation, who would like to see Outward Bound on a hundred college campuses. The Center is proving that the concept is a viable one.

Dartmouth College is an old (est. 1769), small liberal arts college known for academic achievement, athletic excellence, outdoor pursuits and involvement with the surrounding community. Outward Bound arrived on campus just ahead of profound changes: admission of women, integration of racial groups, and year-round classes to allow for a much increased student body without the need for additional buildings. Each student has to spend one term each year away from campus, working, studying or in some volunteer capacity.

Setting up an Outward Bound Center in the middle of a college campus required a considerable amount of initiative to counteract the impression that it is either a survival school or an outdoor club. Outward Bound made a secure place for itself at Dartmouth because it proved that it could offer college students something above and beyond the normal curriculum yet compatible with the traditional role of the university. Strong ties have been forged between Outward Bound staff and the college faculty. Courses are also offered to nonstudents, including an intensive four-week program for older people.

Some of the Center's financial support comes from the Tucker Foundation, named after a former college president. Funds from there go towards programs that "enhance the quality of life in the college, raise issues of conscience, present the student body with opportunities both to reflect and to take action on behalf of conscience, and to further the College's involvement beyond its bounds." If Kurt Hahn ever read these lofty objectives, he must have found them much to his liking.

The Center has no physical plant except a small office and a modest house used for the co-operative program called the Learning/Living Term. The director is Robert MacArthur, a Dartmouth graduate and Episcopalian priest. He had worked in very backward areas of the United States and once, while unemployed, taken an Outward Bound course. This proved to be an unfortunate experience, punctuated by personal conflicts with his instructor, but instead of being turned off, he set out to learn more about the organization, recognized its worth and made Outward Bound his life's work.

The programs at the Center differ radically from those at other Outward Bound schools and yet they adhere faithfully to basic Outward Bound philosophy. There are, for instance, the Laboratories—short sessions to complement what goes on in the lecture halls. Psychology students go rock climbing and sailing, spend a night in a bomb shelter or up in a tree. This helps them to find out how individuals respond to fear, how they can prepare themselves for unusual challenges, what they can learn from such experiences. Students in criminal justice spend forty-eight hours in jail under carefully monitored conditions that compress the time prisoners usually live there. This includes appearing before a parole board, submitting to searches for contraband, and other normal prison experiences, all designed to give students an idea of how the system works—or doesn't work, as the case may be.

· The most imaginative program is the one called the Learn-
ing/Living Term, which consists of a dozen college students
living together and sharing some specially designed classes in
anthropology, drama, education, environmental studies, history, psychology and criminology. Before the term begins, students go on a seven-day wilderness trip so that by the time they
take up residence in the campus home, they are already a
community. The special demands of communal living and the
shared academic work further strengthen their fellowship. During the term there is a Solo and several other expeditions; each
member of the house must also do a service project with children or senior citizens. Since the intense experience of the L/L
Term requires a certain maturity, students must have attended
university for a full year before being accepted.

The L/L Term has developed into an attractive alternative to
campus dormitory living. Letters received by Bob MacArthur
from former students echo the sentiments expressed to Captain
Fuller by former Aberdovey boys: "I have learned about
myself and about people on a deeper level during the L/L
Term than I did during the rest of my years at college"; "We
have lived, we have learned, now let us carry it on—to life."

By 1967 Outward Bound schools were opened in the South-
east and the Northwest. At the **North Carolina Outward Bound
School**, base camp and campsites are hidden in the lushly
wooded Appalachian Mountains and Smoky Mountains,
which, though not on the same scale as the Rockies, provide
some of the finest rock climbing in the United States on the
sheer walls of steep gorges. This school is famous for the highest, toughest, scariest ropes course anywhere. In addition to the
more usual Outward Bound activities there is great emphasis
on observing the rich plant and animal life met on the trail, and
on meeting some of the mountain folk—descendants of the ear-
liest American pioneers—who have retained much of the folk-
lore of their forefathers. The school has made something of a
specialty of intensive adult courses lasting nine or ten days into
which a great deal of living and learning is compressed.

The **Northwest Outward Bound School** sends its all-mobile courses into some of the wildest river, peak and glacier country of Oregon, Washington and Idaho. Students do mountaineering and ski mountaineering in summer and winter, and there are special river expeditions for adults. Service to the community sometimes means joining firefighters to combat a forest blaze.

The newest is the **Southwest Outward Bound School**, which uses as its classroom parts of New Mexico, Texas and Arizona. Students are introduced to desert and canyon expeditions and to river-rafting trips. The school's latest venture was a Himalayan trek in Nepal for adults.

Each of the seven American schools is completely autonomous, having its own board of trustees and the power to solicit funds, recruit staff and students, and publicize its program. Outward Bound Incorporated, the national umbrella Organization, co-ordinates some of these activities. There is also a small organization of school directors who meet occasionally to compare notes and ensure against a parochial attitude in their schools, which are, after all, isolated from each other by great distances.

CANADA

North of the forty-ninth parallel, the Canadians developed two Outward Bound schools—in 1969 and 1974—on middle ground between the British and the American models. The sparkplug in the effort to bring Outward Bound to Canada was Art Rogers, an engineer and mountaineer who had worked for two years at Eskdale—"the most vital and satisfying period of my life," he remembers. He came back to Canada resolved to build a school as similar to Eskdale as possible yet with a distinctive Canadian identity. Together with Mike Perry, who had been an instructor in several Outward Bound schools around the world, Rogers searched for a site: it had to be close to terrain rough enough to make summer and winter expeditions a real challenge, yet safe enough for unaccompanied expeditions, and have reasonably easy access. They looked for peaks and rock faces of varying degrees of difficulty and a river or lake for canoeing and kayaking. Many times they had to fight the temptation to settle for a nice cheap piece of property and then fit a program around it.

A 187-acre parcel of valley bottom available for leasing near the small British Columbia town of Keremeos seemed to fit their requirements. With the help of an enthusiastic management committee, $13,000 was raised and made to stretch like the proverbial widow's mite. Tents were made from locally cut lodgepole pines and quantities of canvas, and discarded church pews served as seats. The kitchen was a trailer, the dining room a collection of odd tables under a tarpaulin shelter, and the sanitary arrangements a six-holer. Plywood sheets were made into shower stalls, cunningly constructed to shield users where it matters most.

It was to be three years before permanent buildings were built, but by then the **Canadian Outward Bound Mountain School** had been granted a charter from the British Trust and was flourishing. The first director, Maj. John Hasell, had been chief instructor at the British Army Outward Bound School, and his habit of writing meticulous reports offers a detailed look at the problems of starting a new school: "It seemed that everything we had begged, borrowed or scrounged arrived on time, but everything we had ordered and paid for promptly was subject to delay, worry and frustration." But there were many joyful discoveries recorded, too: crags rising steeply for 5,000 feet, vertical slabs, overhangs, chimneys and other features to delight the mountaineer; as an afterthought, Hasell mentioned a fairly large population of rattlesnakes.

Hasell quickly found ways to use whatever features the area presented and incorporated them into the program. To introduce students to the school, for instance, he led them on a "quiet walk"—a sort of mini-immersion route. They crossed the Similkameen River—not over the bridge but underneath it,

The Canadian Mountain School, tucked between river and mountains

(Canadian Outward Bound Mountain School)

The best thing about the Canadian Mountain School, in the Okanagan Range of the Cascade Mountains, is its choice of peaks and rock faces to climb.

(photograph by Don Cohen)

Kayaking in the turbulent Similkameen River on the school's doorstep ranks a close second.

(photograph by Ray Preece)

along the struts and over the wooden barrel pipe of the flume or wooden irrigation channel—forded ice-cold streams and muddy backwaters, battled thorny underbrush, climbed up small rock faces and slithered down scree slopes.

Winter courses started in 1971 and proved that the young Canadians gloried in meeting challenges. The first such winter adventure offered them the lowest temperatures in years, broken-down vehicles, frozen water pipes, frostbite and base camp accommodation in two crowded trailers. In spite of or because of this, they came back happy and have been followed by a steady stream of students who sign on for more of the same: sleeping in snow caves or tents dug into the snow at high altitudes, ski mountaineering and cross-country skiing. During avalanche drill, a real live instructor is buried and students have to find him or her, preferably in time to prevent frostbite and asphyxiation.

The question of how to arrive at a viable Canadian identity was on everyone's mind. The British influence continued strong with the next two school directors, who had both started their Outward Bound careers at Eskdale. It is to their credit that they adapted to the Canadian environment and Canadian students, and brought in Canadian staff as soon as such people became available. Some of the components of Outward Bound in Britain—inter-patrol competition, marks given for tidiness, and the more organized activities—disappeared because the youngsters felt these were too much like school or summer camp routines. Physical exercises, too, were dispensed with because the instructors were convinced that a route leading up and down a couple of mountains required enough endurance, speed, balance, strength and courage from students to make athletic training superfluous. Courses were offered to people over thirty, to executives, teachers, military cadets and younger children; to the Standard Course were added short-term programs designed for specific groups.

Patrols from the school travelled farther and farther into the magnificent surrounding country. They went south into the United States, east into the other ranges of the Rocky Mountains and finally into the Far North.

Just as the Canadian Mountain School was at first strongly influenced by Eskdale, the **Canadian Outward Bound Wilderness School** in Ontario was patterned on the American model. Its first director was Bob Pieh, who had started the Minnesota school just one day's paddling from the Canadian border. He looked for the same sort of lake and river country and found it at Black Sturgeon Lake, 100 miles north of Thunder Bay. Unlike the Mountain School, which had to be started from scratch, the Wilderness School fell heir to a ready-made camp, an old Forest Insect Laboratory which they rented for a token fifty dollars a year and the promise to maintain it. The cluster of buildings is set in a sunny, open meadow surrounded by wild strawberry patches and groves of spruce. Almost vertical bluffs for rock climbing and a fine choice of rivers for kayaking and canoeing are close by. It is isolated yet accessible over dirt roads.

Bob Pieh transplanted to Ontario most of what had worked so well at Minnesota, even terminology—base camp became Homeplace, the small groups are called brigades. One of his most ingenious adaptations of an Outward Bound tradition was the Marathon, which in most schools is simply a long run. But, Pieh reasoned, in schools where students are on water more often than on land, this would not be appropriate. So the Marathon at both schools starts with two people rowing a canoe for five miles, portaging it for one mile, orienteering for one mile and running the last six miles.

Using the selection, preparation and packing of expedition food as a learning experience is another innovation borrowed from the Americans. Brigades are handed a booklet containing nutritional values of different foods, suggested amounts and substitutes, along with a list of provisions stocked at Homeplace. It is entirely up to the students whether they are well-fed

Expedition by dog sled at the Canadian Outward Bound Wilderness School

(photograph by Brian A. Back)

Surviving a winter course at the Canadian Wilderness School means taking your water bottle, gloves and boots to bed with you.

(photograph by Brian A. Back)

or hungry since there is no such thing as a convenient corner store where they are going. The staple is "jerky"—strips of beef baked very slowly at low temperature, a modern version of the sun-cured jerky made a long time ago by the local Indians who taught it to the *voyageurs* and *coureurs des bois* travelling these same rivers.

At Homeplace, too, meals are in the hands of students. Those brigades that happen to be staying for a day or two take their turn at cooking, with sometimes interesting, occasionally annoying results. One evening while I was there, dinner was several hours late because the cooks had planned to make shepherd's pie but had neglected to thaw out the frozen meat ahead of time. The seventy or so hungry people milling around the dining hall passed the time recalling their own culinary disasters.

The difference in attitude between the Mountain and the Wilderness schools was described for me by two young instructors, Don Cohen, a Canadian correctional worker and mountaineer, and Korean-born Yujin Pak, table-tennis champion, philosophy student and Rhodes Scholar.

"The Wilderness School is looser than the Mountain School," Don observed. "At Keremeos we considered that the intensity of the experience the students had during the course was enough to make an impression, that it didn't need to be rehashed. If problems came up, we discussed them, if support was needed, we gave it. But there was no specific period when the instructor said, 'let's sit down and talk.' At the Wilderness School we continually emphasize the group process; there is less direction and more freedom to improvise. This takes some getting used to."

"It also means that the program here may not be quite as efficient as at the Mountain School, and that seems to me to be a good thing," Yujin contributed. "Of course a lot depends on the age of the students. The younger ones need more guidance and they certainly gain from the experience, but they may not be aware of it at the time. The older people know what they are getting and usually also where they are going. Many of them welcome the change and the chance to have a go at something quite new. For both kinds of people we have to talk about what we are doing, not just do it."

Superimposed on the two basic models—U.K. and U.S.—are some very distinctive Canadian features. One is the potentially explosive "French fact" that has to be considered wherever Canadians from the different provinces meet. Many young Quebeckers are militantly *French*-Canadian; *English*-Canadians, on the other hand, often see little point in learning French, which is hardly spoken in their part of the country. The result of this language barrier was apparent in one brigade I met at the Wilderness School, in which unilingual youngsters displayed their political sentiments in no uncertain terms. A couple of Ontario girls sported big "One Canada" buttons while the students from Quebec had pasted *"Vive Québec Libre"* ("Long Live a Free Quebec") on everything that could take a decal. But the closeness of living together in a brigade, the shared exertions of the trail and the exhilaration of successfully negotiating difficult rapids and confusing waterways worked wonders. At the end of their course, all the young people had become at least partially bilingual. They had learned to talk together and no doubt to trust and understand one another. Kurt Hahn, who always wanted disparate people to know each other, would have approved.

And, too, the Canadian schools make imaginative use of their gigantic "backyard." Students on winter courses at the Wilderness School learn to travel with a dog team in the northern woods. In early summer, before the plague of mosquitoes and blackflies has hatched, they make thirty-five-day, 500-mile journeys north to James Bay.

In 1978 the Mountain School branched out with a "satellite" course in the Yukon. The instructors and the equipment came from Keremeos, but the students were northerners, several of them Indian. They ventured into country that was uncharted from every point of view. Although the staff were far from their home base, they provided their patrols with everything that spells Outward Bound, as one instructor describes: "Talks by the instructors on canoe hazards, combined with the distant roar of water for emphasis, brought home the serious nature of the Ross River. There was no doubt, right from the moment that the students were required to climb into the icy, waist-deep water and line their boats through the first rapid [walk them through on ropes], that they were very much responsible for their own actions. They knew then that the results of inattentiveness or careless behaviour would be wet and cold. Under these conditions the staff was constantly amazed by the potential of these now alert young people. Again and again they surpassed all expectations of their canoeing abilities."

Highlight of the course was an initiative test: the students were taken across a lake by canoe and left there with instructions to build themselves something to float back to camp on. The vessels that eventually appeared at the campsite were something to behold. A photograph of an "eight-man" craft shows two half-submerged youngsters with the rest "somewhere below."

Chapter 6
People Make
the Difference

The grand-scale geography of North America has had a major impact on Outward Bound. Even more important, however, is the kind of person who arrives at the American and Canadian schools, and their motivation for going there. In Britain, and in most of the British-inspired schools, ninety per cent of the students are sent to Outward Bound as part of their job training; only ten per cent decide for themselves that they would like to go, and are prepared to pay their own fees. In the United States and Canada the ratio is reversed: only about five per cent of the students are sent or ordered to Outward Bound, most frequently by correctional services or a benevolent foundation. The rest believe that a course at Outward Bound is just what they want or, in the case of the younger students, their parents think so and offer to pay the fees.

Josh Miner developed something he jokingly calls Miner's Law: "Check who signed the application form. If the mother's name appears as the signatory, you can be sure the kid really wants to go; if it is the father's signature, then very often it was he who thought the boy should have this experience, that it would make a man of him." (That Miner neglected to mention girls in his Law is a forgivable omission. After all, Outward Bound had begun as a male preserve, but that is another story which will be told in chapter 9. Here I will say only that male and female students now come to the North American schools in equal numbers and are taught by as many female instructors as male ones.)

Oddly enough, Kurt Hahn was quite suspicious of the process of self-selection. He always maintained that being *sent* to Outward Bound was one of the best things that could happen to a young person, that it was exactly those people who would never venture into its orbit of their own volition who needed it most.

The opposite view is held by North American administrators: they argue that young people who *want* to come will get more out of a course. Most of them are already in good physical shape, have had a taste of skiing, swimming, sailing, camping or hiking, and have probably been to summer camps. What they look for are adventure, exciting expeditions, challenges. If they are high school or university students, they have probably earned some money by doing summer, weekend or after-school jobs; if they are already in the work force, they earn good wages. In either case, they have access to money which they are happy to spend on an Outward Bound course.

The young persons who are sent to North American Outward Bound schools, often as an alternative to jail or some other place of detention, come from very different backgrounds. Their poverty ensures that they are in poorer health and probably have had little if any outdoor experience; few of them can even swim. They have had to struggle so hard just to survive in the urban jungle from which they almost invariably come that the idea of creating adversity in order to overcome it is totally beyond their comprehension. To them the "Great Outdoors" is not exhilarating but scary.

Probably the greatest difference between people who are sent to Outward Bound and those who come voluntarily is that the latter feel free to ask questions, reserve the right to disagree if they dislike something, and even walk out on the course if they want. An apprentice whose firm pays his fees considers the cash outlay as part of the expenses required to train him and accepts the program as such. He knows that a report will be sent by the school to his firm and that this report goes into his file, along with those from his foreman at the plant. He is not likely to jeopardize his chances in a tight job market by rocking the boat.

Most of the North American youngsters like nothing better than to rock the boat. This attitude is born of the culture they grow up in, a culture in which traditions are often set aside, or at least modified.

One such "sacred cow" is the ceremony of morning assembly, flag raising and formal prayers that started the day at many Outward Bound schools in the early years. This has no part in the North American schools, but gathering for a devotional or inspirational purpose certainly has. Not always in the mornings, and never the same from one day to the next, these "happenings" provide a change of pace, a short pause before or after the often hectic day. They may consist of readings from one of the adventure or outdoor classics, somebody's thoughts on the day's news, an impromptu guitar solo or a couple of minutes' silence. Sometimes these offerings can set the tone for the day or even the whole course; or they can be of no consequence at all. I have stood shivering on an early winter morning, stamping my feet in the snow, and wondered what on earth we were doing, at that hour, in that temperature, listening to a bit of prose that was totally unrelated to the long, arduous day ahead. But I have also leaned on a sun-warmed rock at suppertime to hear the halting, deeply felt words of a young woman

"The wall." Everyone has to climb it, but how does the last person manage?
(Canadian Outward Bound Mountain School)

talking about her first night on Solo. She spoke of her terror of being alone in the wilderness, which gave way to the serenity of being by herself for the first time in her life.

Hand in hand with this freedom to improvise, to "do one's own thing," goes the practice of self-analysis and introspection. In the North American schools, it is not considered enough to have had a great—or bad—experience. Looking back upon it, discussing it, learning from it, is what makes it valuable in the long run. Peter Willauer of Hurricane Island is quite firm about this: "We feel that an important part of the experience our students have had here has to do with the spiritual dimensions of what they have been through, and the opportunity to examine these in some depth."

Invariably students want to know how and why Outward Bound works. Everyone is made aware that much research has been done on the subject but that no one has come up with a clear-cut answer. The best that instructors can do is to point out that the idea appears to be a sound one, that important things happen to people under stress and that Outward Bound provides challenges different from those met in everyday life. This is always a good starting point for discussion, particularly after a harrowing week in a crowded boat.

Even though the majority of young Canadians and Americans who come to Outward Bound have some acquaintance with the outdoors, they may be quite shaken by their concentrated experience of the wilderness at these schools. Derek Pritchard, director of the Minnesota Outward Bound School, believes he knows why: "Most of them suffer from option shock. At home they have too many options, too many choices, too much available in neatly wrapped and labelled packages. In the woods, the choices are limited, and making wrong decisions has an immediate effect—you lose your way, go hungry, overturn your canoe and get everything you have in it soaking wet. It's an eye-opener to them."

Wendy Pieh, program director at the Canadian Wilderness School, identified the same learning process: "At first students think that I should be *giving* the course, while in reality they ought to be *taking* it. There is a difference. These people say, 'I've paid for this, now you provide me with the experiences and they better be good.' Then I have to try to show them that with such an attitude they'll get little out of Outward Bound."

Instructors have to impress upon students that they are not teachers, father substitutes or cops. They never say, "I'm going to teach you," but rather, "Here are the things I want you to learn. I can't teach you self-confidence or ingenuity in solving problems, but I can point the way for you." As Wendy explained, "We have to know when to stand back and let things happen. Some students respond to that, others have to be pushed a little to deal with what's in front of them. We must not run over our group with an iron fist or give the impression of knowing it all. Most of us are still working on ourselves—I know I am—and we should allow the students to know that."

Another important consideration of the North American program is adequate free time, as Eliza Cocroft of Hurricane Island pointed out: "Not every minute has to be programmed. After all, this is supposed to be nondirective education. Many of the kids don't know what to do with free time because the systems of education they come from don't require them to think. We shouldn't fall into the same trap by throwing so much at them that once again they don't have to think, only to do. Let's see what happens when one fine morning we tell them they are free for the rest of the day." And she added with considerable feeling, "We w/o's [watch officers] need this too, need to learn to pace ourselves so that not every hour is filled with sixty fully packed minutes, every day with twenty-four crowded hours. We seem to work at high pitch all the time and come back from expeditions quite exhausted. We've got to find a few minutes out of every twenty-four hours to be by ourselves to do whatever we want—go fishing, wash our socks or just look at the clouds."

Among themselves, staff members often discuss the question of how much stress students should be subjected to. They realize that instructors must have a keen awareness of actual danger as distinct from perceived danger. Actual dangers are always around the corner. Perceived danger is felt by the student who is off balance, unsure of being able to cope, away from home and thrown into close company with total strangers. In a sea school, for instance, watch officers must balance the two kinds of danger very carefully. Their own knowledge of the sea, weather, coastline and boats enables them to decide what errors of judgement are admissible. If a mistake in navigation has caused a boat to be sent in the wrong direction, they must know precisely how long to let the situation develop before intervening.

One watch officer described an instance of perceived danger in graphic terms: "Our watch had run into dense fog. The navigator was supposed to plot the course to a certain island, but when we approached land, we heard breakers where no reefs or cliffs were marked on the chart. The watch kept noodling around in the fog, quite baffled. We w/o's had to make up our minds how long to wait before sticking our noses into this affair. *We* knew where we were, so we kept silent. The watch then decided to anchor for the night and wait till daylight to find out where they were. Only when this decision had been taken did we tell them where we actually were and discuss how we got there, who had made the decisions, who had not participated in the decision-making but was now participating in the griping. It was a valuable lesson and a typical Outward Bound one."

The students are not the only people who learn something of value at Outward Bound. Instructors, too, know that they are undergoing a significant experience. They take their work very seriously and deal with each other's viewpoints in a frank and open way. From the beginning of my odyssey through Outward Bound, I had wondered why it was that I was able to make almost instant contact with the staff in all the schools I visited, had been accepted by them and made to feel at home from the moment of my arrival. I very quickly felt free to ask them searching questions, certain that the answers would prove to be thoughtful and to the point. At the Canadian Wilderness School, I sat down on the sandy beach of Black Sturgeon Lake with instructors Don Cohen and Yujin Pak and wondered aloud why this was so.

"Because what we are doing is 100 per cent of our life now, all of it, not just a slice of our day as an ordinary job would be," Don offered. "I guess we are the kind of people who reject or ignore a lot of norms accepted by society. We don't aim to take out a mortgage on a house or get rich, at least not yet. In a way we are still searching, not yet ready to go into the Great Melting Pot; maybe some of us never will be. Right now this life suits us because riches to us mean a wealth of people to be with, rather than things to accumulate. Maybe it's not what happens in *real* life, but maybe also that's what we all need— something that takes us out of the ordinary daily round. Outward Bound gives us that opportunity."

He had a point. Since Outward Bound is in a sense "out of this world," the normal period people require elsewhere to get acquainted is not necessary. I actually felt it might be an affront to attempt the usual preliminary small-talk.

Yujin had thought about this: "It's hard to explain but I think those of us who work here breathe a certain kind of air, need a certain amount of freedom in a place that isn't too structured, so we too can grow, not just the students."

"Are you drifters?" I wanted to know.

"Definitely not," both men replied. "We are very purposeful and professional," said Don Cohen. "Almost everyone has a university degree or is working towards one. We come from or go back to people-oriented rather than profit-oriented jobs— social service, work with delinquents, teaching, nursing."

This comment, I decided, pinpointed a characteristic of people involved with Outward Bound. Most of the directors who have guided the North American schools since their beginning have been university graduates with a strong humanistic outlook—rather like Kurt Hahn. If they have not been to university in their younger years, they often enrol as mature students. Invariably, the men and women they choose as instructors are of the same calibre, having the same interests and ideals. They appreciate the freedom to tailor courses to suit the kinds of students who come to Outward Bound, and are not at all unhappy that there are no written rules to follow. Perhaps the closest they come to having a "recipe" is their understanding of something Outward Bound calls "the group process." It moves through the following stages:

1. When students are first gathered together into a brigade, watch or patrol, they make polite conversation. Each person remains in his or her stereotype—the hearty male, timorous or flirtatious girl. They may share some of the same values but only peripherally. Conflict of any kind is usually absent.

2. Goals are starting to be defined: students discuss why they are here, what they hope to gain. Group identity is still low though cliques may form. Students rely heavily on instructors.

3. Power dynamics emerge: members attempt to influence each other, struggle for leadership, compete with each other. Conflicts arise, with the strongest, most skilful people coming out on top.

4. A constructive, co-operative period follows. Members of the group feel confident enough to listen to each other, become more open-minded. Leadership is shared by the group rather than delegated.

5. In the final stages, the group experiences real unity. This leads to mutual acceptance and cohesiveness. Best of all, everyone is in high spirits, recognizes the value of what they have been through, feels a kinship with one another. They have shared the depths and the heights, and they are "high" on the experience.

This kind of relationship is not created readily. A long expedition is the best way of achieving it.

"You need more than just a few days to learn the potential of yourself and your group," Don Cohen told me. "On shorter trips the end is always in sight; on longer ones, nonessentials are stripped away and one gets to the basics. It is then that we have to know when to push, and when to hold back so that students can decide for themselves how much more effort they are able to make. It also gives us time to understand people's feelings, which can run pretty deep in times of stress."

Shepherding a group through this experience is a constant challenge for the instructors, complicated by the necessity of keeping the safety of their students in mind at all times. In the kind of country through which they move, that can be a heavy responsibility.

On the other hand, success can be very rewarding, as Lonnie Nicholls found in leading a course at the Minnesota school. Her encounter with the four boys and four girls in her brigade—all between eighteen and twenty-two years of age—perhaps sums up the Outward Bound experience in North America.

Lonnie had some specific ideas in mind when she welcomed them in the small clearing a few miles from Homeplace where their bus had dropped them. She herself had just come from a winter of nursing in the intensive care unit of a California hospital—a most demanding and stressful job—and knew that some of the young people in her brigade had also been through anxious times such as high school and university exams and problems at home.

"I have planned a physically strenuous course because I think we all need to rest our heads and stretch our bodies," she explained to me. "But it will also be a time to live in harmony with our environment, not at odds with it. I want us to move through the wilderness *gently* and not disturb it—not the lichens on the rocks we climb, not the beaver dams in the little streams on our way, not the bushes and low branches in our path. We won't leave a trace of our passing, not even toilet paper because

The "trust fall"
(North Carolina Outward Bound School)

The North Carolina school boasts the highest, most frightening ropes course anywhere.
(North Carolina Outward Bound School)

we'll use moss and leaves. We'll travel hard but we'll take time in camp to talk, find out about each other: why we've come here, what we hope to get out of the course, what we can learn from each other."

Lonnie and her assistant instructor, law student Bob Fletcher, began to take the measure of their brigade during the very first hours on the "quiet walk" to Homeplace. They noted how the youngsters fared fording a couple of streams, climbing over windfalls and boulders, wading through a swamp. They tried them out in a "trust fall," when each person dropped off a small cliff onto the clasped hands of the others standing below. Did the stronger help the weaker? Did they grumble when they got wet and dirty? Did they share the blueberries they picked, avoid stepping on wildflowers? Did they look about them, or chatter about inconsequential things?

The brigade stayed for the first five days at Homeplace, working their way through the more routine parts of a typical Standard Course. They learned to paddle kayaks and canoes with some efficiency, climbed up and down a few rock faces, practised first aid, took their turn serving and cleaning up meals. They all approached with some trepidation the ropes course strung 100 feet high in the tall trees, but managed most of it without too much trouble. Only young Jim from New York utterly refused to take the "flea's leap"—a jump from a small perch halfway up a tree down to two lower platforms. Ronald, a handsome young man from the Deep South, proved to be the most fearless and agile of the group, though two of the girls, the smallest and slightest as it happened, were not far behind. Everyone climbed up the rope ladders; swung into a net; negotiated wobbly logs, the one-wire traverse, two-wire postman's walk and three-wire Burma bridge, and came yodelling down the zip wire.

Then off they went to the provision store above the kitchen to choose and bag the food for a long expedition. Because of the ban on cans and bottles, menus had to be made up from legumes, grains, nuts, cheese, dehydrated vegetables and fruits, soup, pudding, drink mixes, spices and the makings for trail bread—one and a half pounds of food per person per day. They stowed everything into the distinctive square Duluth packs, which fit tightly into the canoes, added drastically reduced personal belongings, sleeping bags, tarps and maps, then were off for seventeen days.

It was while the brigade was paddling until their arms ached, hefting the canoes over portages and making camp in the dripping bush that some interesting developments occurred, as Lonnie recalled later. "Jim continued to be a problem. He was afraid of going through whitewater and endangered the others in his canoe with his unpredictable behaviour; he tried to cover up his shortcomings with fast talk or by disappearing when every hand was needed. Halfway through the expedition the brigade went on Solo. We put Jim on a little island in a lake and there he completely panicked. When I checked him after the first day, he was a wreck, leaning on a stick pretending to be hurt, then pretending to faint and, when that didn't work, screaming at me. I gave him another few hours alone before pulling him out, but imagine my surprise when I arrived and found him sauntering to the water's edge, hands in pockets, whistling. Sometime during the past twelve hours he had discovered that his fears were groundless, that those scary noises were made by harmless little creatures, that the darkness was lit by a new moon and that he could make himself quite comfortable. He stayed on Solo the full three days and nights, and from then on he wasn't afraid of anything and really enjoyed the expedition. I believe he became a different boy who will carry something of that confident feeling with him wherever he goes from now on."

Ronald, too, had a change of heart in the course of the journey. His looks and background were like a living advertisement for "black is beautiful": he came from a super family, had been to excellent schools, played on the first teams, won a prestigious scholarship to a great university. The rest of the brigade took his bragging for some days and then they rebelled.

An early morning paddle, when silence is instinctive and the only landscape colour is shades of grey

(photograph by Bob Jickling)

They were sick to death of hearing about his achievements, of being shown and told how much better he could do everything, of watching him take charge all the time. It all came to a head at the end of an experiment that Lonnie and "Fletch" tried out. The brigade had travelled continuously for thirty-six hours. Everyone was lightheaded and exhausted but they kept going. Only Ronald fell asleep in the bow of his canoe, nearly causing it to swamp. Lonnie was well pleased with the outcome of this novel marathon: "We drew the canoes up on a little beach and stayed right there for a whole day to talk over what we had just done. All barriers were down—we were too tired to hedge around—and we finally got Ronald to realize that when you are endowed with special qualities and a fortunate background, you have to learn not to flaunt your superiority and not to belittle everyone else. Everyone has their weak spots, as he had himself discovered a few hours ago. He would just have to give the others some credit too."

In time the eight young people had ironed out their differences. They had learned to navigate their heavily laden canoes through the labyrinth of waterways, overcome the city dweller's fear of being alone in the wilderness, stopped worrying about the effects of being outdoors for seventeen days without a hot bath and a bed, and begun to pull together as a community. They finished the course with an unaccompanied expedition and acquitted themselves splendidly. Lonnie and Fletch had once again made the group process work and sent eight youngsters home happy, fit and quite thoughtful.

The sun had dipped below the darkening Minnesota woods; kayakers and canoeists who had been practising on the lake put on a spurt and came whooping in when Derek Pritchard, the school's director, found time to talk to me. He has seen Outward Bound from every angle: as student, instructor and warden in British and African schools. Now he summed up what it means to him: "All this is a very individual form of education, one that sometimes has an immediate effect for a person, like a change in lifestyle. No doubt there are also people who leave

Outward Bound thinking that nothing has changed for them. But I believe they will all in time dip back into the bag of goodies they have carried away from here and pull out something useful. I believe this with my whole heart; otherwise I wouldn't be doing it, wouldn't have done it all these years."

Derek paused for a minute and then said quietly, "You know, this is our gift to the students. We work extremely hard and give an enormous amount of thought to the matter of giving those who come to us an opportunity to grow and to go away with just a little more than they arrived with."

On another evening, Eliza Cocroft of Hurricane Island had said something similar to me: "It is up to us to see that these young people get a sense of joy out of the program, not only a sense of fulfilment and of accomplishment. This sense of joy is what makes Outward Bound so different and what we must guard with everything we've got."

Chapter 7
Meanwhile, Back in Britain

Time has not stood still for Outward Bound in **Britain**. It is always more difficult to change traditions than to start out new, but the British schools of today have moved with the times. They have opened their doors to women as well as men, to people of varying ages and backgrounds, to groups from many countries. They have adapted to the very different generation of young people now growing up.

Nowhere is this more noticeable than at **Aberdovey**, as I discovered on a sunny summer's morning in 1979. We formed a ragged circle outside the grey stone mansion which is the core of the school, to listen to a student—obviously not English—stumble his way through the news and weather report. We are a motley crowd, standing, lounging, sitting by our packsacks: brown and black faces among the white (or sunburned flaming pink); the harsh sounds of Arabic mingling with English spoken in half a dozen accents from around Britain, from Bermuda and from Canada. There are youngsters on the Standard Course who are still in their teens, a group of oil company apprentices from Abu Dhabi on the Persian Gulf who must be in their twenties, half a dozen senior executives from the Avis car rental firm who are well into their thirties and forties. The girls among us are more or less indistinguishable from the boys except that they fill out their jeans and T-shirts a little more. Ian Fothergill, warden of Aberdovey, is somewhere around too, part of the crowd.

The day before, I had taken tea with Captain Fuller in the small house to which he retired after a distinguished career at sea and then with Outward Bound. We had talked about Aberdovey as it was in the beginning and leafed through his collection of "historical" photographs, several taken at the exact spot where I was standing now. Closing my eyes, I conjured up the scene as it must have looked in those wartime years: the very English-looking lads (no girls) dressed alike in navy jerseys; tidy rows facing the flagpole and the Union Jack; marches in formation down to the docks, supervised by Merchant Navy captains in their smart uniforms; crisp commands, ringing "Sirs" and readings out of the Book of Common Prayer. An extraordinary contrast!

I saw in my mind's eye, too, the paternal figure of Kurt Hahn, his face half hidden beneath a floppy hat; Dr. Zimmermann, bald pate gleaming, making a remark in his fractured English; the towering figure of Lawrence Holt; Freddie Fuller fresh from his ordeal in the South Atlantic, and Jim Hogan worrying whether the clouds scudding across the sky over the Dovey Estuary heralded a change in weather.

I jolted myself back into the present and observed Ian Fothergill. Curiously enough, he does not appear far removed from his predecessors. A big man whose relaxed manner hides the tensions that characterize a virtual workaholic, he has a geography degree and has had experience on an Antarctic expedition. It is also quite obvious that he has the same amount of zeal and devotion to Outward Bound as the men he succeeded. He may

In contrast to the uniformed, disciplined, boys-only student body at Aberdovey in the early days, today's students in Britain are a relaxed crowd of boys and girls. This group is at Eskdale; Warden Roger Putnam stands at bottom right.

(Outward Bound Trust)

glance back over his shoulder now and again, but mostly his eyes are firmly fixed on the present and the future.

"We can still run on the enthusiasm of Kurt Hahn," he reflects. "We still aim to touch the hearts of our students, but we need more subtlety to bring home the lessons. Our main object always was to teach an attitude that would help people survive rather than survival as such, but in those early days this was easier and the aims were clearer."

Outward Bound has come a long way since "those days." The road has been rock-strewn and in the early 1970s nearly came to an abrupt end. "We had some traumatic periods," Fothergill acknowledges, "primarily because we had not moved with the times. We were happy to welcome the apprentices but failed to realize that industry had changed. We used to be able to sit back and wait for students to turn up in satisfactory numbers. Ours was a take-it-or-leave-it attitude; when it dawned on us that they were leaving it, we finally sat up and took notice."

There was good reason for the complacent attitude with which Outward Bound had cruised along for so long. The name had found its way into the everyday vocabulary of the English-speaking world. Although outdoor and wilderness education centres proliferated in the postwar years, they never caught the public's imagination as Outward Bound did. Sending apprentices to the schools became established practice in many industries, and among outdoor centres Outward Bound itself became Establishment. Until 1967 a steady 5,000 or so students passed through the British schools year after year.

Then enrolment began to decline. In 1973 the government slashed budgets and industry went into recession, cutting the work week and freezing wages. The immediate outcome for Outward Bound was the cancellation of 2,500 sponsored students. Outward Bound's existence hung by a thread and draconian measures were necessary to prevent the thread being snapped.

"We had to change our image," says Johnnie Johnson, who

is director of marketing. "We attacked the problem from several sides. Since most of our students came from industry, we asked leaders of the business world and from the trade unions to serve on the Trust. They made it clear to us that we must set up a partnership between industry and Outward Bound. In particular, we had to recognize that the calibre of the training and personnel managers, on whom we relied to send us apprentices, had changed. Many of these used to be ex-Army, Navy and Air Force officers who heartily approved of us. But now a new breed of men occupied these positions. They had to be convinced that we could do something for their firms to justify the £700 in fees, lost time and wages which it cost them to send one apprentice. They wanted to have a dialogue with us about the courses we offered. They questioned the length of the Standard Course and the age of the young people we accepted, citing the fact that they mature earlier nowadays, something we had not fully acknowledged. They wanted our staff to write a different kind of end-of-course report. 'We are not interested in how well a lad sailed a dinghy but whether he had shown or developed qualities which would benefit our company,' they said."

The new men on the Trust put their expertise to work on behalf of Outward Bound. Arguing that the best committee is a committee of one, each person on the Trust made himself responsible for specific areas of the organization—buildings, finances, publicity, recruiting—and worked exceedingly hard to improve these areas.

Some of the changes made were drastic. The lease on the Devon school ran out and was not renewed. Urban encroachment rendered the Moray school less attractive and it, too, was closed. Outward Bound took over an existing outdoor centre at **Loch Eil** near Fort William in the Scottish Highlands and turned it into a combined sea and mountain school. **City Challenge** was successfully introduced to more urban centres.

The most basic alterations were made in the courses offered. Although the Standard Course remained the backbone of Out-

Britain's large urban centres offer a different kind of challenge. Here, Outward Bound students teach children to read.
(City Challenge)

ward Bound, contract courses became increasingly important. Length and content were tailored to specific clients. Executives over twenty-five years old were offered programs lasting from a long weekend to two weeks. Whole classes from British and French public and private schools came with their own teachers who doubled as auxiliary instructors. Teachers, police cadets, mountain leaders and sailors arrived in satisfactory numbers because courses were designed to be of particular appeal to them.

The school at **Ullswater,** under its longtime warden, retired Squadron Leader Lester Davies, pioneered special programs for children. Beginning in 1972 they offered the Discovery Course of fourteen days for boys and girls fourteen to fifteen years, an eight-day Mini Course for youngsters ten to thirteen, and a six-day Midgie Course for eight- and nine-year-olds. The staff at Ullswater make a point of introducing these children to most of the activities found in the Standard Course. Discovery, Mini and Midgie programs, they insist, are not watered-down Outward Bound courses but the real thing modified for younger age groups. Ullswater boasts another unique feature: a 120-foot-long floodlit plastic ski slope where students do something called jet skiing. Since the area has more and longer-lasting snow than other parts of the Lake District, there is snow skiing and even some igloo building and "snow-holing," which are activities sure to thrill children and make them candidates for other Outward Bound experiences in the future.

To lead these new kinds of students, a new type of instructor had to be found: men and women with not only academic training and outdoor skills but also the ability to relate well to young people, to give them choices rather than orders.

Everyone concerned with the new Outward Bound was acutely aware that the strongest assets of the old one had to be retained so that its distinctiveness from other outdoor centres was not lost. Whatever the length of the course and whoever the participants, the basic Outward Bound core was included: the residential situation, the action-centred leadership, the small groups, stepped-up physical challenges, the insistence on discipline and self-discipline and the translation of the Good Samaritan parable into some form of community service.

The **Army Outward Bound** schools, too, had to find ways of adapting their programs to the young people reaching maturity in the 'sixties and 'seventies. In the Welsh centre, the young soldiers and apprentices were met at Towyn railway station by wartime commando hero Jack Churchill, who "played" them back to the school with a bagpipe solo. From there on, however, it was all rock climbing, athletics and expeditions. The basic program was expanded to train British and Commonwealth officers and NCOs as potential instructors in outdoor activities. A second centre for members of the British occupation forces in Germany was opened in southern Norway near Christiansund, with a winter base camp in the Telemark Mountains. These Army Outward Bound programs provided the peacetime army with some interesting variety in their training as well as combatting the boredom that inevitably creeps into their ranks. A new focus to their activities was required and what better way than Outward Bound, that "moral equivalent to war"—a phrase coined by the American philosopher William James and appropriated by Kurt Hahn.

The blending of the old and the new has been accomplished particularly happily at **Rhowniar** which, together with Aberdovey, is designated **Outward Bound Wales**. There is a special feeling about Rhowniar—someone called it the school with a soul. It is housed in a distinguished old mansion that has been lovingly restored, new wings merging with the original building. Nothing has been allowed to intrude on the peacefulness of this sanctuary between the sea and the hills; even the two ropes courses are cunningly concealed in the immaculately groomed grounds. The deft touch of Warden Wendy Johnson is discernible everywhere—in the attractive way meals are prepared and served, in the low-key atmosphere, even in the storage rooms and equipment sheds with their neat racks of wetsuits, rows of canoes and shelves of climbing gear.

The gracious mansion in the Lake District that is home to the Eskdale mountain school

(Outward Bound Trust)

Although now coeducational, Rhowniar started out as a girls' Outward Bound school, and staff brought to the new set-up much of their expertise in understanding the needs of women students. Wendy Johnson, who spent many years as a physical education teacher in Britain and the United States, and as chief instructor at Rhowniar before becoming warden, adds her own special approach. She meets all students, takes the measure of each patrol, and then allows her staff and students to take it from there. No two courses are ever exactly alike.

"I don't feel strongly about such details as morning prayers or readings," she says. "Sometimes they're nice things to do when we feel like it. We've never had the early run-and-dip on a regular basis either. As a matter of fact, we wonder whether it is physiologically right, especially if people have to be browbeaten into it."

What Wendy Johnson and her chief instructor, Keith Choules, do feel strongly about is the Drama Program. I was curious about this because I had heard it mentioned in scathing terms by one or two Outward Bound people to whom the word challenge means hiking fifty miles in rough country or paddling a kayak through churning rapids.

"Drama is a totally different sort of challenge," Wendy explained "Some of the people who come here, especially the boys, cope with physical demands quite well. It's easy for them to rappel off a cliff or deal with a sail flapping in a stiff breeze, but when you ask one of these tough guys to get up before a crowd and give a two-minute speech, he stands there shaking in his boots. Contrast this with the person who finds the ropes courses really frightening and yet when it comes to putting on a ten-gallon hat and pretending to be a cowboy, he shines. Pretty soon both sorts of people realize their own strengths and limitations. I can assure you that the drama productions we put on are really equivalent to the final expeditions. We invite local people and parents to the production and it becomes one of the highlights of the course."

Rhowniar offers very well-rounded Outward Bound courses.

The rock climbing, sailing, canoeing and overnight expeditions are there, but so are the workshop where a fleet of surf canoes are being built by the students, the theatre for dramatic productions, the nature study classes and the group discussions.

Tacked on the notice board in the staff room are letters from students, all starting with "Dear Wendy." Nothing demonstrates better how far Outward Bound has come than this simple salutation. It would not have occurred to the students in the earlier years to address the warden in so familiar a way. Yet this familiarity does not change the respect that staff and students have for each other. "Dear Wendy" is looked up to as much as "Sir" was in the past.

"We had 1,500 students go through Rhowniar last year," Wendy Johnson told me. "That is 1,500 people whose lives have been touched by us—a sobering thought."

Chapter 8
Not Quite
Blood Relations

The far-flung and loosely connected Outward Bound family
has had to contend with a number of near-relatives and even
one or two who do not belong at all but only pretend to do so.

IN NIGERIA

In 1951 an outward bound-type school was opened at the
historic anchorage of Man O'War Bay in what was then the
British Cameroons, later to become Nigeria. There, a far
greater proportion of time than in the British schools was
devoted to community service: building trails and bridges and
initiating self-help schemes for the surrounding villages. Training for citizenship and leadership was stressed, in keeping with
efforts to emancipate Africans and prepare them to run their
own affairs. For the first time in the history of this huge, mul-

tiracial territory it was possible for members of different tribal associations to live and work together: "Moslem and Christian, northern Arab, southern Yaruba and Ibo; camel men with canoe men, city clerks with farmers," writes David James in his book *Outward Bound.*

Following Independence, this school became the Citizenship and Leadership Centre, with a mountain school at Shere Hills and a sea school at Apapa. By 1980 these schools had become an important force in the country. To keep the students' experiences alive when they return home, Man O'War Clubs have been organized in several communities, schools and colleges. They, too, stress character-training through adventure and service to the community.

IN SOUTH AFRICA

The mixing of the different races, which was so successful in Kenya and Nigeria, was not possible in South Africa when the idea was first suggested in the 'fifties. Since Outward Bound has always been deeply committed to this policy, the Trust could not grant a charter to a school that would practise apartheid. However, there were enough interested people in the country by 1958 to establish a parallel organization called the Veld and Vlei Adventure Trust. The noted explorer, soldier and author, the late Freddy Spencer-Chapman, became warden of the first courses. He reluctantly agreed that to press for multiracial courses at that time would have been to scuttle the program before it ever got started.

Initially, the idea was resisted by some, as the school's founder J.L. Omond explains: "When I first proposed an Outward Bound school, I met with criticism; it was felt that South Africans got enough fresh air activities because of our good climate. I assured my critics that many of our people spend much of their leisure time *inside,* in a pub, the cinema, at home, and that all our population could do with more outdoor activities."

Today, Veld and Vlei supports two programs in Cape Province and one in Natal near the Drakensberg Mountains. Courses are given only during the winter and summer school holidays since ninety-five per cent of the trainees are schoolboys. A few all-girls courses are included each year but no coed ones.

South Africa offers challenges peculiar to its geographical location. Patrols have been variously known to go without water for a whole day and to find a small stream running among their sleeping bags; to wake to six inches of snow on their bivouac and to swelter through heat registering 104°F in the shade.

Until 1979 Veld and Vlei literature, which closely resembles Outward Bound brochures, was written in Afrikaans and English. Now it comes also in Xhosa and Zulu, which are two of the seven main languages spoken in South Africa. According to Omond, in the summer of 1979 the first multiracial courses were held, with government blessing. This drew teams from radio, TV and the print media to report on how black, white and coloured students and staff shared not only adventure but also tents and showers. They worked so well together that all those involved pronounced the course one of the best ever held.

To be able to advertise multiracial programs, Veld and Vlei had to amend its constitution. It can now also apply for an Outward Bound charter from the Trust if they wish.

IN HAWAII

Hawaii Bound has not been sanctioned by either the British Trust or Outward Bound Inc. in the United States, and has no charter. Yet it was started with the help of American Outward Bound schools and staff, its literature is indistinguishable from that of the American schools, its program is similar and its current director held the same position in the Minnesota school. Tom Price, a former warden of Eskdale and one of Outward Bound's philosophers, recently spent three weeks at

Hawaii Bound. He remarked on the closeness with which this school adheres to the precepts of compassion, service and physical fitness emphasized by Kurt Hahn.

Established in 1975, Hawaii Bound adapted to the singular topography, climate and society of these Pacific islands. Base camp and most of the courses are on the island of Hawaii, usually referred to as Big Island. Camps are made on the beach, in lush jungle and on the barren uplands devastated by gigantic lava flows. Essentially a benign environment without poisonous plants or dangerous creatures, the islands can come up with enough challenges to satisfy most Outward Bounders. Volcanoes can erupt without warning, tidal waves and tropical storms can transform the balmy seashore into a storm-whipped hell. Rock climbing is virtually impossible on the crumbly volcanic cliffs, but the ingenious instructors have found a way around that: they teach rappelling off a bridge and down a deep canyon wall. Hikes to the top of the highest volcanoes— 14,000-foot-high Mauna Loa and Mauna Kea—require clothing and equipment normally unnecessary in these latitudes. Students have to guard against sunstroke and dehydration as well.

Hawaii Bound makes use of the island mystique and language whenever possible. The programs try to provide a link with Hawaiian culture and history rather than impose an alien one. For instance, the small group is called an *Ohana,* a term that Tom Price feels reflects the great emphasis the school places on imaginative personal growth: "The terms 'patrol,' 'watch' and 'brigade' are drawn from enterprises in which the individual comes second to the task at hand, in which adventure and rigour are inherent and in which the emphasis is on the male. *Ohana,* on the other hand, stands for the care and protection of the individual, integration of people into a cohesive, intimate, caring unit which makes its own demands, in a way, upon the courage and spirit of the individual. Patrols, watches and brigades evoke comradeship, *Ohana* evokes love."

Special to Hawaii Bound is the fact that most students come from the islands and do not lose sight of each other or of the

At Hawaii Bound, the *Ohana* takes responsibility for the individual and for the group.
(Hawaii Bound)

Students climb from the seashore, through tropical jungle, to the tops of 14,000-foot volcanoes.
(Hawaii Bound)

To the surprise of youngsters, the police in Bermuda run outward bound-type courses.

(Bermuda Police Force)

staff at the end of the course. Members of an *Ohana* may be tied by blood as well as by shared experience. If one member is in need, the others are compelled to respond, in the present and in the future. Student and staff differences or problems are settled by calling a *ho'oponopono*—a gathering of *Ohana* members: "an inspiration, no less," in Tom Price's enthusiastic words.

IN FRANCE

La Guilde Européenne du Raid has an outdoor centre near Lourdes on the Spanish-French border. Their prospectus could be a translation of any Outward Bound brochure and even shows a picture of Eskdale entitled "the English school," implying a direct relationship. Courses for men and women eighteen to thirty years of age are twenty-six days long. Students come from all socio-economic backgrounds, and are taking the course to "improve personal courage, work in small groups, have contact with nature and go on a Solo to provide time for reflection, development of imagination and enthusiasm." There is mountaineering and skiing in the Pyrenees, caving, canoeing, mountain rescue drill and athletics.

IN BERMUDA

"Catch them young and train them well" could be the motto for members of the Bermuda Police Force who run an outward bound-type program for young children on their island. Bermuda is compact and densely settled; tourists come ashore in droves, and there is hardly any open ground or stretch of beach that is not already overused. Not very promising territory upon which to plant Outward Bound, perhaps, but Sergeants Lynn Hall and Bob Porter and their colleagues are determined cops. For a short while each year they have the use of Paget Island, which is otherwise used as a training centre for delinquents. Boys and girls mostly between twelve and sixteen years come for eight days and are given an abbreviated Outward Bound experience. They learn to climb up and rappel down a forty-foot crag and then apply what they have learned on the slightly higher St. David's Head. There is canoeing, sailing in a lugger, orienteering and even some community work on Paget Island itself and at the two hospitals in Bermuda.

Money is raised to send youngsters to British Outward Bound schools when they are old enough to take the Standard Course, and a few of the policemen themselves also make the trip to learn more about Outward Bound. I met one of them, Bob Porter, at Aberdovey where he was dividing his time between being a student and an assistant instructor. He told me that the youngsters in Bermuda are usually surprised to discover that the program is run by policemen. The scheme seems to be good public relations for Outward Bound and for the Bermuda police.

IN COLOMBIA

Groups of young men from Colombia have been coming to the German *Kurzschulen* for some years now to take Standard Courses. In 1978 Ulf Händel, director of the Baad school, was invited by the German embassy and the Colegio Andino, a German school in Colombia, to visit the country, help choose a site and generally advise on the possibility of establishing Outward Bound. Händel had a marvellous time travelling throughout the country. In true Outward Bound style he found adventure in unlikely places, stumbling on a smugglers' camp, sleeping in a hammock, surviving close encounters with poisonous snakes and scorpions. But he did find a site that seemed ideal, in southern Colombia near the small town of Pitalito. Within easy reach of this possible base, students could take expeditions on horseback, climb in the mountains, travel in jungle, and canoe or raft down the Rio Magdalena.

One of the problems which will confront an Outward Bound school in South America is recruitment of students. In general, the young people selected to go to Germany have been from wealthy families and there is a strong possibility that these are the same ones who would take advantage of any school in their country. This could mean that exactly those youngsters who need Outward Bound most would never come within miles of it.

Ulf Händel has submitted his report; now it is up to the Colombians to act upon it.

IN JAPAN

Sketchy information about a potential Outward Bound school in Japan has trickled in. So far the school consists of an office in Tokyo, printed stationery, a preliminary report and a steering committee. When courses become a reality, the Japanese islands should provide splendid sites for kayaking and canoeing, skiing and climbing.

THE ONES THAT GOT AWAY

It is not surprising that imitators have tried to leap on the successful Outward Bound bandwagon. Unfortunately, those who do not recognize the fine line between a real Outward Bound school and an outward bound-type school, relying solely on the magic name to attract customers, sometimes get into difficulties. Without the safeguards imposed by the British Trust, Outward Bound Inc., Outward Bound Canada and the other national bodies, these undertakings can be dangerous; more commonly, they miss out on the underlying Outward Bound philosophy which gives a purpose to outdoor activities and adventure centres. Problems with several such imitators have made Outward Bound administrators very conscious of the need to protect the good name of Outward Bound and to make sure that organizers of new schools are fully aware of everything the name stands for.

Chapter 9
His, Hers, Theirs

All Outward Bound schools have "the wall"—a fourteen-foot-high, smooth wooden structure which students have to climb over without touching the edges. This requires teamwork, strength and agility. The Canadian Mountain School built two walls, "his" and "hers," the latter a few feet lower. But ten years later, "hers" still stands unused. Predictably, or surprisingly, depending on whether you view women as the weaker sex, neither all-girl nor coed groups have given it a second glance.

Outward Bound cannot really be faulted for having been a male preserve to begin with. After all, it was founded for the benefit of young males in their most formative and problem-plagued years. Instructors have always recognized the peculiarities of adolescent boys: their swings between bursts of energy and periods of lassitude, their lack of social graces, and unwillingness to take responsibility. These insecurities mark a watershed in the adolescent's life; a slight push can send him in one direction or another. Outward Bound's purpose has been to supply this push in a constructive way and help boys over these essentially self-centred times to a clearer view of themselves and their fellow men. Any problems girls might have in that period of their lives were considered only as an afterthought. Jim Hogan did arrange a few "rather limited" courses for Sea Rangers at Aberdovey in the 1940s, and reports that the girls acquitted themselves very well indeed; but not till the early 1960s was Rhowniar established as a girls' school and were coed courses cautiously introduced in the United Kingdom.

The British schools were not by any means alone in their male orientation. In American schools, the question of whether to admit girls was only resolved after heated debate. The first program to include women was offered at the Minnesota school. Bob Pieh, the school's founder and first director, pleaded for their inclusion on the grounds that, after all, they are people too. He remembers vividly some of the arguments against having women: "The most vehement one was that if women did as well as the men, it would diminish the mystique of male superiority. Allowing women in on an equal basis would be bad for the male egos, especially if by any chance the men ever came off second best. Nobody seemed to be concerned for the women's egos. The legend that Outward Bound was a rugged outdoors kind of thing had to be preserved, not made easier so that women could do it, too. In the end it was reluctantly agreed to 'give Bob a chance,' but I was cautioned not to make women too independent."

Shortly after this, a lengthy workshop was held at the Colorado school solely for the purpose of deciding whether to allow women students to take part in its courses, and under what conditions. Needless to say, the first coed experiment went like a charm. None of the fears was realized: the girls did not lag behind; they carried their share of the loads; they did not freeze on rock walls, or turn all coy at the toilet and sleeping arrangements.

Up or down, it's a great way to go.
(Hurricane Island Outward Bound School)

In North America, the first women instructors did not have to ask for concessions from the male-oriented Outward Bound. The male staff discovered that there were any number of women as well or better qualified to be instructors.

Marion Schaffer, a petite instructor at the Canadian Mountain School who often leads all-male patrols, explains the impact of this discovery on her students: "I come as a surprise to the men arriving here. They are all psyched up for a tough course and it's a real letdown when their instructor is a woman, especially one who, like me, is so short they tower over her. At first they feel they have to show off. Of course, I also have to be careful not to taunt them with remarks like, 'If I can do it . . . if you can't keep up with me . . . .' It is not my job to make male students feel less masculine because I do something better. Mind you, it is also not my job to make special efforts for the women students except to get them to do whatever the men do.

"Sometimes the men think they'll have an easy time with me, and then I really have to push hard to overcome that. My main goal is to have a good course and I don't want to jeopardize that."

The problem of male/female roles is perhaps the most sensitive issue. Liz Horne, a sturdy Scot, a mountaineer and physical education teacher who has led all-men, all-women and coed groups at the Canadian Mountain School, looks at it this way: "At Outward Bound we can find out what it is like to be treated as an equal, but we will only *be* equal if we leave any preconceived ideas at home. If I go on a course saying to myself, 'Of course I won't be able to keep up with the men, of course I may not be able to make it to the top,' then I have lost the opportunity to find out if I really can or cannot. This can happen if a male student wants to move faster, thinks the girl is holding him back, and offers to lighten her pack or encourages her to take an easier slope. If a woman has trouble with a ski binding, she may be tempted to ask one of the fellows to fix it for her or allow one of them to volunteer to do it, because she is so used to asking for help. This is a way of conning women into playing a stereotype role, and we instructors have to see that it does not happen. Without interference, a woman will usually make it on her own."

At the beginning of coed courses, the men try to inject a spirit of physical competition, to put on a show of superiority. This usually lasts only until they realize they don't have to prove anything. They see that being big and strong is of secondary importance and anyway is often compensated for by the women's better balance and co-ordination.

The women, for their part, discover that using brute strength is not the only way to accomplish a formidable task. How well I remember the terrible time I and another woman had portaging our kayaks through the northern Ontario bush. We were nearly in tears from aching limbs and frustration at lagging so far behind the men in our brigade. The brilliant idea occurred to each of us at the same moment: "Let's double up and carry our kayaks in relay." One at either end, we made good time and had both kayaks in the next stretch of water with everyone else's.

Earlier that summer, a watch officer at Hurricane Island had made the same point to me: "Women could do a lot more if they used their brains instead of bemoaning the fact that their arms aren't very strong. Maybe it takes three of us to pull in the mizzen or the sheet, but we can do it and do it right."

The men and women on coed courses soon become aware that in times of stress, a person's real qualities become highly visible. It is not necessarily the men who deal more uncomplainingly with hunger, wet or fatigue, whose powers of endurance are superior, who co-operate better with each other. Sometimes a skeptical male will sit back and wait for a female to fall flat on her face, but not often. Most of the time he will be impressed by her valiant struggle to cope, and by the fact that she complains less than her male compatriots. And both men and women soon realize that whereas men tend to take their achievements for granted, women seldom do.

One of the unexpected discoveries for women on an Outward

Just inches off the ground, even the wobbly log can be a challenge.
(Canadian Outward Bound Wilderness School)

Bound course is that there is no need to defer to men or allow them to take the lead in tricky situations. Hurricane Island Watch Officer Eliza Cocroft feels it is the w/o's duty to see that women in mixed groups assert themselves: "Because women do not easily take to leadership, they hang back and wait for situations to sort themselves out. When they are encouraged to make decisions, they sprout confidence and a great awareness of their potential, like tropical plants after a downpour. As one woman put it to me fervently, 'If I could only be this alive in my mind back home.' "

A small bonus in coed groups is the toning down of swearing and similar behaviour normal in all-male groups, for men realize these are neither necessary nor desirable.

Courses for women only can be even more valuable than coed ones. Becky Pierce, watch officer on the first women's course at Hurricane Island in 1971, remembers it as a wonderful experience. "We had two watches made up of a few young girls, six women in their forties and six in their fifties. They all worked extremely hard, helped and supported each other in times of stress, and managed imaginative meals on the rather basic food we carried. We w/o's did a bit of handholding and we all got emotional a few times, but we worked things out without any of the group hassles we sometimes get with men's or coed watches. The women's motivation was fantastic—they had really wanted to come, sometimes in the face of considerable opposition from their menfolk. For some it was the first time they were able to escape from the stereotype female role they had played all their lives. Their most urgent need was to explore the many other sides of their personalities, to find avenues leading to personal growth."

Yvette Cardozo, a Florida writer, describes a similar intensity of experience. Many of the twelve women in her group seemed to be on the brink of change. They had been separated or divorced; had seen their children leave the nest; had gone back to work after years at home, or were thinking of doing so. "We had chosen the women's course because we did not want to be with men during this experience. It was important to avoid competing against them or falling back into deference to them. This was our time to be women among other women. The result was that emotions ran higher, there was more soul searching, more sharing, and more crying. We were experiencing the stress that all Outward Bound students experience, but unlike the others, it was totally new. We were discovering our physical beings for the first time, discovering the ranges of our emotional capacities and discovering just how capable we could be" (*Adventure Travel Magazine,* June 1979).

I can personally testify to one item on the Outward Bound agenda as having a salutary effect on mothers and housewives. After years of propaganda promoting germ-free this and spotless that, the experience of walking, clothes and all, into a black, oozing bog is enormously exhilarating. I had joined a brigade just starting an Outward Bound course in Minnesota. We had been told to wear our oldest clothes. The instructors collected watches and billfolds and put them into a small pack, which would be transported to Homeplace while we went for a "quiet walk." After some bushwacking, a little rock scrambling and fording a couple of creeks, we headed straight into a swamp. The first few steps came as a surprise—wet slime squelched into my running shoes and grabbed my pants bottoms. By the time only my head showed above the rank, clinging goo, I had passed from a state of shock to disbelief and finally to utter bliss. Something joyful was happening to all of us. Being uniformly filthy was sensationally unifying. We started to play, to fling gobs of guck at each other; we took little side trips to explore floating islets, laughing and shouting with glee. I remembered how my children had revelled in making mud pies and stepping into puddles, and resolved that when I have grandchildren I will not become angry with them when they get filthy. The ten soggy people oozing black muck finished their "quiet walk" by wading straight into a lake; they were not the same ones who had started out in clean clothes a few hours before. We had all learned something, and I believe I had learned the most.

Women instructors and students bring a touch of grace to a group. On Solo they may build a little nest for themselves; their campsites are usually neat, with perhaps a flower arrangement to soften the harsh environment—something to feast their eyes on. But these things in no way interfere with their ability to do what is necessary. Men can learn a lot from women, and on Outward Bound courses, they often do.

This is a recurring theme. Outward Bound is not only a matter of overcoming physical obstacles and meeting challenges; there is so much more. An appreciation of wild flowers, of the interplay between plants and sea creatures at tidewater; time to look inward; a growing sense of belonging to a new kind of community—these discoveries are all part of Outward Bound. The women in a group are usually the first to recognize this, and by their joy and happiness transmit the feeling of wonder to their male companions. Women are also sensitive to their own and others' feelings, and much more able than the men to be open about them. In the close proximity of an Outward Bound group, men not only allow themselves to feel—they probably do that all along—but also to show these feelings.

The subject of sex has to be dealt with, too. At the Canadian Mountain School, Director Adrian Todd often talks to the incoming students about it, especially if many of them are young people. He says that friendships between boys and girls should remain platonic, that the course is supposed to be a group experience, and that any pairing off is bound to be disruptive. For the same reasons, he prefers to split up married couples between different patrols. Keeping them together does not work very well because they represent a separate unit, dependent upon each other rather than on the group as a whole.

Problems sometimes arise when there are fewer females than males in a patrol. I temporarily joined two patrols on a winter course which included one and two girls respectively. In the first, the boys initially referred to Jennifer as "the girl" and expected her to do the cooking on the expedition, but she soon cured them of this attitude, and the patrol quickly became a well-functioning whole. Jennifer finished up with six brothers. In the second patrol, the two girls clung together and, try as he might, the instructor never had a cohesive group, but always six boys and two girls.

At the Minnesota school, brigade cabins were built with a partition down the middle at the insistence of some members of the board of trustees who worried about "immorality." At the beginning of a course, men and women segregate themselves in the cabin, but when they return from expedition they find the partition an intrusion and ignore it.

Director Derek Pritchard is aware that the male/female relationships have to be handled with care. "We have to be alive to the feelings of the brigade as well as of individuals," he says. "I prefer not to lay down any policy but to leave it up to the instructors to 'read' their brigade correctly in this regard. Take skinny-dipping, for instance. I don't want to affront anyone's sensibilities or go against the practices of religious groups who frown on this. But I also don't want false modesty carried over from students' backgrounds to the school."

At Hurricane Island, the school's open pulling boats present their own peculiar problem for what in a more genteel age was known as "the call of nature." Students live the best part of a month on the boats and there is nowhere "to go" except over the side. Girls in particular at first don't see how they can possibly empty their bladder or bowels: they feel thoroughly insecure letting go over the heaving ocean, and painfully embarrassed into the bargain. Sometimes they ask for a blanket to be held up, or try to find a little privacy in the lee of a sail if the wind is right. The watch officers show the way unobtrusively. Everyone follows their example and soon nobody cares. Says Eliza Cocroft, "There is no time to worry about it—the environment makes its all-encompassing and all-important demands on you and the small things tend to fall away. You pee when you have to."

How well women are integrated into Outward Bound courses depends very much on the relationship between the sexes in the

The stresses of an Outward Bound course lead to elation and self-discovery.
(Outward Bound Inc.)

At Cobham, women prefer their courses to be as difficult as the men's, but separate.
(Outward Bound New Zealand)

country where the particular school is operating.

The attitude in Canada and in the United States is clear-cut. society is coed, so are we. Men and women work together in the "real world" and so they must in the microcosm of an Outward Bound school. As a matter of fact, they work together exceptionally well. Competition among male instructors is absent, as is any suggestion that women play a lesser role or must come on strong to win total equality.

Most other countries are only beginning to move away from strict segregation of the sexes. Coed courses as they are known in North America are virtually nonexistent in Africa, though a few women's courses are offered. In the Singapore school, the executive courses are mixed, with women taking the same program but sleeping by themselves. On Standard Courses the girls do not have a Solo, mainly because many other people camp on the island of Pulau Ubin and so it is not considered safe. The girls' program is slightly different, with shorter expeditions and longer periods for water survival and capsize drill, "as they tend to panic more easily than the men do." As far as I can find out, no female instructors are employed in African or Asian schools.

The New Zealanders expect women students to be just as tough as their male counterparts. The course program is the same, but groups are either all-male or all-female. Former school director John Mitchell admits that in the early days of a course he is asked why it is not coed, and that at the end the women say they are satisfied they can handle themselves as well as the men, but as a group of women.

In Australia, Garry Richards has been trying for years to make courses coed; his problem is that only one woman for every seven men comes to Outward Bound. A very few courses, mostly those for older people, are coed. The Standard Course is the same for boys and girls, though one exception is made: the ropes course is modified to take into account the greater number of women who are unable to support their body weight by their arms. (Watching Canadian and American girls negotiate the ropes course as well as and sometimes better than the boys, one must conclude that the Australians are observing the results of athletic training rather that a gender weakness. In other words, give girls the same amount of strength training and they will perform as well as the boys.)

In Outward Bound South Australia, Standard Courses are coed, but "only just." Youngsters sleep in segregated dormitories at base camp. On expeditions, however, they are issued two-man tents: the staff do not ask any questions but let the students sort it out themselves.

At the Outward Bound school in Holland, women are not treated differently and the programs are the same for men and women. There are coed as well as single sex courses, and also some female course leaders.

In Germany, courses are theoretically coed, but far more boys than girls enrol. So far, no mature women have taken courses in the *Kurzschulen* and they are not expected to "for another ten years." (When I joined a group of youngsters from the Berchtesgaden school on a vertical rock wall, I was greeted by some pretty skeptical looks. These were replaced by good-natured applause on my arrival at the top in as good time and shape as the youths.)

In the British schools, the ratio of female students to males is roughly one to five, and here, too, there are few female instructors. Because Rhowniar started out as a girls' Outward Bound school and only fairly recently became coed, the staff there have had longer to clarify their approach to girls.

"Boys and girls certainly react differently to given situations," Warden Wendy Johnson has observed. "When you say, 'Go over the wall now,' you'll see the boys take two steps forward and the girls three steps back. You can't say to the girls, 'Jump off that cliff, come on now, don't be a baby.' Instead you have to say, 'Let's look at this now; it's quite safe, and you might think how you feel about *not* doing it when all the others have.' With the boys there is an almost automatic masculine response of 'I mustn't be shown up in front of the lads.'"

The author as Outward Bound student
(photograph by David Wilson)

As a woman I am, of course, very sensitive to the whole question of female students and instructors. It seems to me that allowing the other half of humanity into the schools has enriched Outward Bound immensely. I am also convinced that an Outward Bound course at any of the schools can be one of the best things to happen to a mature woman. Equality of opportunity and ability is taken pretty much for granted by the younger generation, but for us older women it can still come as a marvellous surprise. And it is gratifying to realize that courses advertised by Canadian and American schools for "women over thirty" are actually for women over thirty, forty, fifty.

There is another point that I am happy to make. In schools where the coed system is in full swing, the atmosphere is a loving one. Not in the sense of men and women strolling hand in hand into the sunset, but in the sense of both sexes caring and sharing. I am as little ashamed of using these overworked phrases as the Outward Bound instructors are of living them.

Chapter 10
The Luxury of Time

At Salem and Gordonstoun, Kurt Hahn sent students on solitary walks "to think things over." In a speech given at Oxford in 1938, he described loneliness as one of the health-giving passions: "The love of Aloneness cannot grow up amid the confusing turmoil of incoherent sights and sounds. Neither love of men nor love of God can take deep root in a child who does not know aloneness." *Are we ever alone now w/ computers/tv/radio?*

The purifying effect of solitude has been recognized throughout the ages by many different cultures. Africans and North American Indians use it as part of their puberty rites. Men training for religious vocations have always been sent to meditate in solitude. The record of Christianity and Judaism is full of allusions to disciples going out into the desert to clarify their thoughts. Australian aborigines go on "walkabout." Lord Baden-Powell incorporated a short period of solitude in his program for older Boy Scouts.

Solo is: a snug, homemade "tent"
(photograph by Don Cohen)

In the British Outward Bound schools, a formal Solo was introduced at Eskdale by Eric Shipton in 1953. Youngsters were sent out to stay by themselves for twenty-four hours, not far from the school.

The first course in Colorado featured a twenty-four-hour Solo at a reasonable distance from base camp. The response to this was impressive. Reports that it was the outstanding experience of the whole course were the rule rather than the exception. If a one-day Solo is good, reasoned the staff, a two-day Solo might be better, so they started to experiment with varying lengths. Chief Instructor Ernest Tapley, who is part North American Indian, suggested that the Solo could test the boys' survival skills if they were sent out without food or sleeping bags. Of course, they would have to be taught how to build shelters and forage for food. Another dimension was added when students were encouraged to meditate, possibly fasting as well or at least cutting down on food. Thus the three-day Solo evolved as an exercise in survival and a time for contemplation.

Weather and other environmental conditions determine the type of Solo possible in each school. For instance, three days and nights spent in subzero temperature without food or shelter would be courting disaster. Foraging for food is not possible in most locations: either there is nothing much edible to be found or successive waves of people picking the area clean is seen as ecologically unsound. Even where fasting is advocated, iron rations are always given to students as a matter of course.

Time becomes less important when one is alone. If students do not take along a watch, they learn to live with the clock provided by nature—the position of the sun, the ebb and flow of tides. At first there may be a slight sense of disorientation, a feeling of having to eat and sleep in the familiar pattern. This soon passes as students become attuned to the natural rhythm of the environment.

Joe Nold, who helped to make Solo so much a part of Outward Bound, is convinced of its worth: "It is a compelling experience that stimulates introspection. To those people who feel lost without something to do, I say, 'The Solo gives meaning to an experience of doing nothing: try it. You set your own goals. Ask yourself what would give substance to being alone for three days, with no one to talk to, no one to tell you what to do, no agenda save what you devise for yourself.'

"It is also useful to remember that on Solo you experience the basic essentials of life in their stark reality—hunger, cold, loneliness, fear, as well as a deep calm and self-reliance. It is all happening between you and your environment."

Solo is always closely but, if possible, unobtrusively supervised. At the American sea school and in the Australian satellite course in North Queensland, where students may have an island all to themselves, each day they put up a flag that is visible from the daily inspection boats standing offshore within hailing distance. If no flag is seen, the crew anchor and investigate. Schools in potentially dangerous terrain give students strict instructions not to move farther than a specific, very limited distance from their campsite. If they go near water, they must wear life jackets.

Since Solo is the most unusual experience of the course for most people, its effect on them has been well documented in numerous articles, personal journals and verbal reports.

"I never realized how much I needed people" is heard as often as "I never knew how great it is to be alone." For some active young people Solo can be a real trial. "If they'd given me a trail to build I would have been a lot happier" is the way a twenty-year-old Canadian put it. On the other hand, a housewife in her mid-thirties had never felt more free: "This was the first time in my entire life that I had been quite alone. I married young, had three kids right away. To be able to sleep when I wanted to, to shout and dance around, have no one dependent on me—that was heaven. Perhaps this isn't exactly what Solo is for, but that's how it affected me. The Outward Bound literature talks a lot about personal growth. Well, I think I grew about ten feet during my Solo and I hope I stay that tall."

Doing nothing at all can also make Solo memorable, as I

... an island all to yourself
(Hurricane Island Outward Bound School)

discovered for myself on a small island off the Maine coast. I built a shelter, inspected my little domain, contemplated the tides, the sea birds, the changing skies. I hardly touched my iron rations and didn't bother to dig for clams, though I did use up my three matches to boil some water and taste tea made from bayberry leaves. Although I had pencil and paper along, I did no writing and no deep thinking. Afterwards, I realized that the value of Solo for me lay in taking a complete rest from the intense activity of my everyday life.

City people are sometimes overawed by their patch of wilderness. They want to become one with it, do nothing to disturb it. Never before have they had the time and the opportunity to observe the filigree of a dry leaf, the intricate construction of a wild orchid. They become instant Thoreaus, converting their Solo site into a personal Walden Pond.

Solo exerts its greatest influence on a person who is in a state of personal *un*balance and is therefore more open, more receptive, more willing to examine his or her life and come to a few conclusions. People who have their feet planted firmly on their chosen path are not beset by too many doubts. To them, Solo is much like any other new experience. They make the best of their camp and their loneliness, are philosophical about going hungry and not much disturbed by the strange night noises. They even return a little disappointed. A few people are too distracted by their rumbling stomachs to do more than just wait till they can sit in front of a good meal again. Once in a while, a student will report having entered into a state of euphoria and emerged a changed person.

What Solo does to a person depends on expectations. Someone prepared for an earthshaking experience that does not happen will feel cheated; a person who expects to be scared and isn't feels like a conqueror; one who goes in cocky and discovers fear will be a humbler person.

Ian Fothergill, warden of Aberdovey, sounds a note of caution: "Solo can certainly be a powerful experience, but not always positive; in fact, it can be quite disastrous. I have seen a watch working towards a really good relationship which was ruined when everyone was sent off on Solo. Instead of drawing closer together, these people cut themselves off for a period and never regained the closeness of earlier days. At Aberdovey we leave it up to the instructors to decide when their watch should go on Solo, for how long and, indeed, whether they should go at all. The value of Solo is relative to the value of the rest of the course and depends to a certain extent on the weather, how well the watch has worked together, their age and general disposition. We do not believe that Solo should become a fixed, nonnegotiable period. We prefer to look upon it as a flexible exercise, something that can be a good thing under certain circumstances."

There are nearly as many ways of introducing students to solitude as there are Outward Bound schools. At Hurricane Island, a watch may be dropped off without warning on a bare little island to spend a night in a group Solo, alone but together. At Loitokitok, Solo happens in two stages. Pairs of students make bivouacs at the 14,000-foot level of Mount Kilimanjaro. They sleep one night together to accustom themselves to the loneliness of their lofty eyrie, and on the second night each student retires to his own "bivvy." By contrast, Cobham School in New Zealand pitches its students into Solo in a most unceremonious way, dropping them off a launch at night in Cook Strait. The beach at that point is too shallow for the boat to approach, so the young people have to wade ashore with their equipment, to be greeted by oppossums' eyes gleaming in the darkness. The campsites are totally isolated, each hemmed in on three sides by green bush and on the fourth by the sea. Basic rations are provided, but fasting is suggested and about eighty per cent of the students report doing so. They are allowed no reading matter, transistor radios, sharp knives or fishing gear. They must not swim, and may not move around beyond a fifteen-yard radius. One visiting instructor did a blindfold Solo in that particular location to find out how his other senses compensated for the loss of sight.

. . . disembarking at night to camp on a lonely beach.

(Outward Bound New Zealand)

In Australia, Solo is adapted to the environment. In New South Wales, students camp on the tops of ridges in the Australian Alps. Their spirits are uplifted by magnificent views over vast areas of the surrounding country. Food is supplied in sufficient quantity for their reduced energy demands and for the distinctly contemplative Solo that is recommended. On the North Queensland Solo, there are two choices. Students are dropped off by boat on islands of the Great Barrier Reef. Everyone is provided with drinking water, some basic rations, and fish hooks, sinker and 100 feet of line. A student wishing to go the survival route tries to get by with what he can catch; if the fish don't bite, he can break into his emergency supplies. Or, if he prefers to use the time thinking more purposefully, he can eat just enough to avoid the distraction of hunger pains or the need to catch his supper. School staff place equal value on each approach and leave the choice up to the students; they also do not check on who did what.

Hawaii Bound strongly encourages its students to try a contemplative Solo, which has two variations. They can opt for a mobile Solo during which they may walk around within a 100-yard radius, touch and smell whatever they come across, perhaps write or sketch. The other choice is to move only when absolutely necessary, taking all the time to look inward. Some concessions have to be made to the climate in the way of supplies—a poncho against sun and rain, water and a lemon juice/maple syrup mixture to ward off dehydration. Basic rations are provided, but it is suggested that fasting could enhance the experience.

Veld and Vlei has "Operation Solitaire," during which students are left alone for roughly twelve hours at nightfall. They camp out of sight and sometimes out of hearing of each other in a big circle, with their instructor in the middle in case of emergencies. Even under these somewhat tame circumstances, students find this period awe-inspiring.

To suggest fasting in the middle of winter in Canada would be foolish. Students take along double sleeping bags, the hal to boil water, and some fatty, high-protein food such as sardines or tuna. In the Mountain School, the Solo sites are high up in alpine country; in the Wilderness School, they are in the midst of frozen lakes and dense forest. The snow is very deep and one can get completely lost within a few feet of camp, so students are given strict instructions not to wander.

Among the more alarming aspects of the Canadian summer and winter Solos is the thought of being attacked by a wild animal. It is true that bear, deer, skunks, beaver, porcupines and even the odd cougar share the same wilderness, but these almost always keep to themselves unless disturbed or provoked. Far more tangible to city-bred people is the knowledge that there is no one to communicate with, that the only human voice heard is their own. The sounds of the wilderness can be very frightening—the countless scrabblings of small creatures going about their business, the hoot of an owl or call of a loon, the snapping of twigs and the wind sighing in the treetops. In winter, snow slips off the deeply bowed branches; large and small avalanches sound like thunder. When the days and nights are clear and cold, there is an electricity in the air, a snap and crackle under the high dome of the sky. The shimmer of billions of stars shows crystal clear in the blackness of the night. But when it snows, and the world shrinks to within inches of one's sleeping bag, the sense of solitude and isolation is profound.

In most schools Solo sites are permanent and used frequently, but in Canada students pick their own spots: cosily tucked into the overhang of a cliff; dug into a snowdrift; nestled under the protective branches of a cedar; or out in the open— on the sandy shore of a little lake or by the side of tumbling waterfall. In these surroundings, Solo will be a high point in the Outward Bound experience.

Chapter 11
A Splendid Laboratory

A large number of "adaptive programs" sired directly or indirectly by Outward Bound have introduced the joys of adventure to other groups of people besides the healthy adolescents for whom it was first designed. These adaptations have evolved in three ways:

* Courses are organized and staffed by Outward Bound instructors for specific sponsors.

* Schools, organizations for the handicapped, and correctional services like what Outward Bound does and run similar programs of their own, calling them everything from outward bound-type courses to ordinary outdoor education. Credit may or may not be given to Kurt Hahn and Outward Bound.

who has worked at Outward Bound starts a pro-
is own, taking care to mention the connection.

Where Outward Bound is not directly involved, the high
safety standards it has imposed on its own schools may not be
observed. Yet when accidents happen, the name Outward
Bound somehow creeps into the news reports. This is not a
small problem: in the United States alone there are more than
200 direct imitations using Outward Bound methods and terminology, and 400 schools, universities, correctional institutions
and private organizations offering outward bound-type programs. Troublesome as this can be, the growing number of
adaptive programs is itself testimony to the appeal of Hahn's
original idea. As the British educator Colin Mortlock put it,
"There is no more potentially dynamic form of education than
adventure. Adventure is a state of mind that begins with feelings of uncertainty about the outcome of a journey and always
ends with feelings of enjoyment, satisfaction or elation about
the successful conclusion of that journey."
Adaptive programs have made their greatest impact in three
important areas:

In Education. In the early 1970s a new term was born, "experiential education"—learning by doing. Ninety participants in
the first Conference on Experiential Education gathered at
Kingston, Ontario, in 1973 to talk about outdoor pursuits in
higher education; most of them were connected with Outward
Bound. Four years later their numbers had swelled to over 600
and included individuals and organizations who shared roughly
the same teaching philosophy.

This development was a direct result of research into American education showing that, whereas at the beginning of the
century society was experience-rich and information-poor, the
situation was now completely reversed. What children needed
was practical experience to go with the academic content of
their school lessons: "action learning" to augment "book learn-

ing." This conclusion led to the proliferation of outdoor education programs, first in private schools, in time also in public schools.

In Britain, on the other hand, education authorities had decided in the early 1960s that adventure, within the framework of outdoor pursuits, should be provided for all school children. By 1970, a great many secondary schools were involved in some aspect of outdoor education. Local education boards have set up their own outdoor centres, and the central government has created national centres which train highly professional specialists and also offer outdoor recreation for the general population.

In Canada, both private and public schools have adopted outdoor education in varying degrees as part of their curriculum. A good example is Atikokan High School in northern Ontario. Its "Outers" course runs for a complete school year and includes several overnight trips, one long expedition, a Solo, a St. John's Ambulance First Aid Course and twenty hours of community service.

Outward Bound South Australia has an arrangement with several schools to send whole classes for abbreviated Standard Courses. In Britain, too, children from both private and public schools come to Outward Bound in class groups.

Teachers can become students in special courses for educators at almost any Outward Bound school in the world. The usefulness of these courses is described by one American teacher, Sheryl Hinman, who was able to apply what she learned at Hurricane Island to her classroom in Illinois. She had never set foot in a sailboat until the course and felt very discouraged at her ignorance. On the second day of her Solo, she sat down to write out everything she could remember about sailing and was astounded by how much she had learned. The simple act of writing out what she *did* know gave her such confidence that she now uses the technique with discouraged classroom learners. Sheryl had found much of the Outward Bound course extremely difficult and wanted to give up many times. When she returned home, she talked to a youngster who told her how often he wanted to quit school. "In that encounter I found the strongest reason of all for Outward Bound," she writes. "I now could empathize with a struggling learner. I could look at that boy and say honestly, 'Yeah, I *know* how you feel.'"

Alice Casselman is a Canadian teacher who is convinced that Outward Bound has done as much for her as she has done for Outward Bound. She is a member of the board of trustees of the Wilderness School, a biology teacher and author of a booklet on nutrition that is given to students planning long expeditions. When I met her, she was in charge of expedition food at the school. A year or so before, she had been at a crossroads in her career, in need of arriving at a different perspective and a sharper focus. She took a year's absence from her job to work with Outward Bound, and now knew that her period of uncertainty was over, that she had found what she was searching for and would be a more effective teacher when she returned to her post.

"Outward Bound can be extraordinarily valuable for people like myself," she told me. "I joined a brigade composed entirely of teachers. We realized pretty soon that we were all Indians and not Chiefs as we were used to being in front of a class. That's a salutary thing to discover and makes one rethink one's methods of teaching. We are so used to talk, talk, talk that we forget there may be better ways of teaching—by example, for instance.

"We had one man on this course, a big, flabby, loud-spoken type who insisted on telling the others how to do things. He was also the oldest and so assumed automatically that he knew more and should play teacher to the rest of us. After suffering for a few days, the brigade rebelled. We sat down to a really heavy discussion and made him see that what he had been doing to us, he had also been doing to his own students—not giving them time and space to find out anything for themselves. At the end of the course this teacher was a different man: he

had lost weight, was more soft-spoken and willing to
was also big enough to acknowledge the debt he ow⌐⌐ ⌐⌐ ⌐⌐
colleagues."

With Delinquents—"hoods in the woods." Some of the most
imaginative adventure programs have been devised for the correctional services. Cynics might be tempted to dismiss them as
another out-of-sight, out-of-mind approach by many judges
and magistrates. Not so, says Vick Hines, who runs a wilderness
program for wayward girls in Texas.

He gave me a very clear explanation for the success of these
programs: "Wilderness experience works on delinquents
because for the first time in their lives they are required to pit
themselves against environmental rather than human adversar-
ies. These are young people with a long history of reacting
against authority—parents, teachers, cops, probation officers,
judges. They have been consistent failures. Then they encounter a wilderness camp which shocks them into realizing that
they have to change their behaviour, because nature isn't going
to change. They learn about the cause and effect of living: if
you don't choose a dry location for your camp, collect firewood,
check the weather, look after your feet or take enough food, if
you eat all your food in the first couple of days, then you suffer,
and it's no one's fault but your own. In other words, behaviour
modification is initiated less by people in authority than by
nature itself. The wilderness introduces delinquents to what
Kurt Hahn used to call 'sensible self-denial'—a hard lesson to
learn for people who have a very low level of expectation and
whose goals are geared to immediate satisfaction."

Outward Bound instructors have remarked on the difference
between delinquents and youngsters who have never been in
trouble. The offenders have been sent to the wilderness camp
as an alternative to jail or correctional school. The life they
have previously led may show in all sorts of ways: in small ones
like the lack of compassion and awareness of beauty that allows
them to stamp on bugs and flowers with vicious pleasure; in big

ways like their strongly held, stereotyped view of society. To them, women are sisters, mothers or whores; men are pimps, johns or police officers. Racism, too, is deeply ingrained. Both sexes often hate and fear members of other races. These attitudes can be turned around successfully only if one or two of the girls excel in outdoor activities; if a few boys discover that they like cooking; if they see that being gentle with weaker comrades or wild creatures doesn't hurt their image; that skin colour is not important after all. In addition, youths who start out by boasting about their exploits on the street eventually discover that sailing a boat in a storm is more exciting than stealing a car.

Instructors have also noticed that patrols composed entirely of delinquent youngsters have not been particularly successful, for they do not become cohesive groups, do not create effective leaders or happy followers, and are slower to develop helpfulness towards the weaker members among them. A far better solution is to include one delinquent in an ordinary patrol, as is done at the Canadian Mountain School. No one except the school director knows who that person is; in most cases, the instructors do not *want* to know. This can work wonders with a young person, because, for possibly the first time in years, he or she is treated like everyone else in the group. As I have mentioned, the New Zealand school goes one step farther: the relevant information is sent to the director by the city office in a sealed envelope, to be opened only if there is trouble and he needs to know whether he is dealing with a delinquent or not.

One community program that must have been devised by a genius is the Los Angeles-based Barrio Outward Bound. In a wilderness setting in the High Sierras, street workers bring together leaders of rival gangs. It is invariably the first time these people have ever spoken to each other; in earlier encounters they have communicated mostly with switchblades and other lethal weapons. The experience of living together and sharing very real dangers helps to develop not only gangland peace but actual co-operation between former bitter ene-

Caring and sharing are two overworked words that take on new meaning at Outward Bound.
(North Carolina Outward Bound School)

mies. Using this same method of confrontation in a wilderness camp between people who would normally be at odds with each other, is Manpower Challenge in Colorado. In this experiment, Outward Bound instructors lead patrols composed partly of factory foremen and partly of prospective employees from the ranks of hard-core unemployed men. Each group learns to appreciate the other's strengths and problems, and to recognize the possibilities of working together.

The best hope for a successful rehabilitation is, of course, with the very young offender, as the staff of Enviros in southern Alberta—many of whom have worked at Outward Bound—have discovered. They take children from age fourteen, and a few even younger if they have been chronically in trouble with the law, their families and their school. The Outward Bound model has been modified to take into account the longer program— three months in spring, summer or fall, two months in winter. This is a tough place for adults and children. The long expedition, for example, may take up to seven weeks. Service to the community is stressed; in fact, the whole camp has been built by staff and students. The youngsters are also given lessons in basic reading and writing in the hope that they will become a little more enthusiastic and skilled in their school work.

Vick Hines, the tall, part-Indian Texan whose wilderness camp for delinquent girls is so successful, introduced me to an innovation increasingly used by the more enlightened leaders in correctional work. It is a written contract that spells out exactly what is required of the delinquent and of the staff. It is drawn up and signed by both parties, each of whom keeps a copy. The mere fact of having such a document in their possession, to be looked at whenever they wish, is a unique experience for the young people. Never before have they made written agreements of their own devising, to which both they and those in authority have to adhere.

With Handicapped People. Derek Pritchard, director of the Minnesota school, is in the forefront of those who have adapted

Outward Bound to the needs and capabilities of the h.
capped. "If the concept of Outward Bound is valid," he s..ys,
"then it should be so for all; one just has to fit the experience to
all types of people. I see everyone, from the severely handicapped to the Olympic athlete, as simply having escalating
abilities. If you draw an inclining line, you see that one can get
on it at different points, like this."

Olympic athlete

(median physical ability)

mentally handicapped, deaf,
blind, paraplegic, amputee

BUT sh M
there are classism
issues

Not one to preach without doing, Pritchard has translated his
ideas into practice in various ways and places. At Loitokitok,
for instance, he led groups of blind Africans to the top of
Mount Kilimanjaro. Glaciated at the top though it straddles the
equator, this giant is no Sunday outing even for the able-
bodied. For the blind boys it was an incomparable experience:
"I suppose it never occurred to anyone that blind people might
actually enjoy such an adventure, but they were as exhilarated
by the feel of the snow, the sensation of height and the wind on
their faces as we were by the incredible view."

In the same spirit of "why not?" Derek Pritchard taught
kayaking at the Devon Outward Bound School to children
damaged by Thalidomide, and inaugurated a program for the
severely handicapped at Minnesota. There, men and women in
wheelchairs, accompanied by an equal number of staff and
students, paddled canoes, made portages, crossed swamps and
went on Solos. Some even negotiated parts of the ropes course,
though this meant lifting them from their wheelchairs by pul-
leys to a platform high in the treetops, strapping them into a

A wheelchair need not be a barrier to taking an Outward Bound course.
(Minnesota Outward Bound School)

and sending them down the zip wire.

a group of deaf people, instructors prepared themselves with a crash course in sign language, lip reading and the problems of the deaf in a hearing society. Before the students' arrival, Derek and his staff had to concern themselves with a number of fundamental questions: Should all the deaf students be in one brigade? Should there be an equal number of deaf and hearing people in a brigade, or perhaps one or two deaf and the rest hearing? Should the onus for making them understood be on the deaf, on the instructors or on the other students? Would a deaf instructor be advisable if one could be found or trained? What concessions, if any, should be made?

Derek Pritchard is also aware that handicapped students might take a dim view of being on the receiving end of something suspiciously like "do-gooding": "There is a fine line between making an Outward Bound course possible for handicapped people as a right, and doing it as a service project for the benefit of the other students."

With so many adaptations and innovations around, it is no wonder that Outward Bound is being studied by administrators, educators, correctional workers, athletes, safety inspectors, psychologists, sociologists and other experts. It has become a happy hunting ground for graduate students in search of a dissertation theme.

Outward Bound has also commissioned studies of itself. The granddaddy of them is undoubtedly *The Challenge of Outward Bound,* undertaken in 1968 and published in 1971 by Basil Fletcher. A distinguished educator and author, Fletcher began his research in a distinctly critical frame of mind, "having heard Outward Bound either praised or denigrated in, it seemed to me, extravagant or emotional terms." In spite of his misgivings, he wrote in his report that what had begun as a simple wartime expedient in 1941 had become astonishingly relevant in the world of the 1960s. When Professor Fletcher asked recent graduates whether they thought Outward Bound had influenced them for life, seventy-two per cent answered that they thought it had, and sixty-four per cent of those who had been on a course five years before still thought so.

Six years after Fletcher's study, however, Kenneth Roberts, Graham E. White and Howard J. Parker came to less optimistic conclusions in their book, *The Character-Training Industry*. The title of the book itself was bound to raise the hackles of anyone connected with Outward Bound: although the term "character-training" appeared for many years in Outward Bound literature, it has fallen into disrepute and is certainly never used today. The subject of this research was not only Outward Bound but also a number of other British centres where outdoor education and adventure experiences are offered.

The authors' most serious criticism of the character-training industry was that it could not substantiate the claims that these programs actually changed and/or improved the personality and work habits of the young people: a lot of glowing testimonials, certainly, but no hard facts and figures. There are, for example, the foremen and factory managers who for decades have sent apprentices to Outward Bound but seem vague about exactly why this is done. They gave various reasons: "It gives the lads a different view of life and discipline . . . the lads take a different attitude to authority . . . they come back with more confidence in themselves . . . strong discipline is good for those who have rejected authority . . . they tend to be a bit more loyal to the company." Some admitted that they hoped there would be a financial gain for the company in increased productivity of the apprentices. Others sent people who deserved to be rewarded, or those who needed their rough edges knocked off. All agreed that an apprentice who refused to go to Outward Bound was looked upon with disfavour.

These assessments are important to consid large percentage of the young people who c Bound and similar centres are sent there industry is concerning itself increasingly with and less with only partially understood humar

In their conclusion, the authors paint a

picture for the character-training industry unless it can attract clients from a much wider circle than the business world. This could include using the centres for straightforward recreation, as a place where delinquents are rehabilitated, or as part of the general education system. (As I have already mentioned in chapter 7, Outward Bound has since made many important changes and its schools are once again fully booked.)

Almost every research study carried out in North America during the last few years forecasts a bright future for Outward Bound. People of all ages are coming to it in large numbers— nearly 8,000 per year in the United States, more than 1,000 in Canada—because they are promised *real* adventure in rugged surroundings, and the opportunity to stretch their minds and bodies beyond anything they have previously experienced. For Outward Bound to continue to prosper, it must offer programs that are a lot more challenging than those available from the hundreds of summer camps and outdoor clubs in the two countries.

Outward Bound is shown to be at its most successful when it demands the utmost from its students. In a study charmingly entitled *The Reason for Freezin'*, A. Donn Kesslheim of the University of Massachusetts School of Education maintains that the value of Outward Bound lies in its offering a sharp contrast in the environment as well as the benefits of stress, provided they do not appear contrived. People, he says, respond most positively in a new and unfamiliar environment. Experienced sailors get less out of a course at Hurricane Island than from one at the Colorado school.

Although it is never easy to measure human responses accurately, various tests have been devised that come close. For a Master of Education thesis, Simon Fraser University student David Hopkins took a group of young people on a four-week mobile course in the Cascade Mountains of British Columbia, giving them proven self-concept tests before and after, taping conversations and reading logbooks and diaries. Hopkins concluded that there was a statistically significant increase in the students' self-esteem and self-assertion. "The stress of group

living within the rugged environment helped
to discover more about themselves and what
of," he wrote. "It allowed them to release e
sonal potential which the constraints of eve
disguise."

One aspect of the Outward Bound Standard Course that is
much debated these days is its length. Is the twenty-eight-day
format really the best or would a shorter one do as well? Is
Outward Bound's message and effectiveness being diluted by
three-week or even two-week courses? These are extremely
important questions in light of the current Outward Bound
practice—invariably imposed on reluctant wardens and directors by head office administrators—of shortening the courses.
Many British instructors insist that "you are lucky if you get a
reaction in under a fortnight," and that "it is in the last week of
a twenty-eight-day course where the best work is done." This
contrasts sharply with at least one American study using psychological testing of students which indicated that most of the
change seems to take place in the first two weeks.

Only one conclusion is constant in all the growing stack of
research papers: virtually everyone who has taught an Outward
Bound course can explain very well *what* he or she was doing,
but not so readily *why*. All they can say for certain is that, for
whatever reason, it seems to work. Garry Richards, director of
Outward Bound Australia, says it rather well: "People who
have experienced Outward Bound exude a confidence border-
ing on faith. Since it is difficult to analyse faith, it is also
difficult to analyse how and why exactly Outward Bound
works."

Perhaps it is not so very important to know why. I am
tempted to agree with a little verse by e.e. cummings:

> While you and I have lips and voices which
> are for kissing and to sing with
> who cares if some one-eyed son of a bitch
> invents an instrument to measure spring with?

Chapter 12

More Beyond

Surely not everything about Outward Bound can be drawn in
glorious technicolour: are there not any darker tones in the
picture? Of course there are, and people in the organization are
well aware of them. In spite of the tremendous enthusiasm
Outward Bound has generated, the vivid comments and wide-
spread support, students are not always thrilled with the program. In Minnesota I had the opportunity to read evaluation
reports written by students: "A waste of money . . . too much
emphasis of the physical . . . too much discussion and talking
. . . too much stress on group involvement . . . a contest of how
much pain and misery one could bear before breaking down
and crying" were some of the remarks. No doubt similar ones
can be found in reports handed in at most of the schools.

Staff members, too, have their doubts. Purists among them
feel that Outward Bound needs a moral shakeup, that there is a

Former Eskdale warden Tom Price with future instructor Dini Biggs
(Canadian Outward Bound Wilderness School)

double standard in a few of the schools. They po
tors who have been known to carry their own—b
expeditions, to sleep in snug tents while their students spend
uncomfortable nights out in the open, to drink and smoke while
enforcing the no drinking, no smoking ban for students. The
other side of this argument is, of course, that students come for
a limited period and instructors should not have to subject
themselves to the same conditions month after month, year
after year.

Traditionalists do not like the current trends to shortening
the Standard Course and offering Outward Bound courses to
the very young, the middle-aged, the handicapped and the delinquent. They argue that Outward Bound is not and should not
be for *everyone,* that it can only lose its potency by spreading
itself too thin.

Is it better to employ full-time professional instructors, or
inspired amateurs who come and go? The debate is heated. In
the Alps, professional guides are a solidly entrenched tradition,
and both German schools consider them necessary for the
safety of their students. In Britain, wardens say permanent staff
give the schools continuity and stability. North American
schools argue that well-qualified amateurs come with a fresh
outlook and tremendous enthusiasm which cannot be matched
by full-time instructors.

Outward Bound offers adventure and some risk—obviously a
drawing card for the many thousands of people who enrol. But
there is the obverse side to this coin. Outward Bound schools
usually locate in the most rugged landscape they can find, and
their programs include *potentially* dangerous activities. Even
the most rigorously enforced safety standards are occasionally
inadequate or not met, because of either human or mechanical
failure. Outward Bound administrators are understandably reti-
cent about the number of fatal accidents that have occurred,
but considering the hundreds of thousands of people who have
gone through the schools since 1941, there have been astonishingly few. As far as I can find, these are the statistics.

In Britain, the record has been exceptional: in nearly forty years there have been only six deaths, most of them due to exposure in rapidly deteriorating weather. The United States has had thirteen deaths—several by drowning and by exposure during winter courses. In Canada, one young man died of heat stroke; another by drowning in shallow water, having wandered away from his Solo camp. Hong Kong has had four deaths, two from lightning strikes. Singapore lost one man who collapsed while running the Marathon, and another who was discovered to be fatally allergic to a hornet sting. In Malaysia, two men died during or after the Marathon and two by drowning. Australia lost six students, all in the same disaster when a sudden storm swamped their boat. In New Zealand, a rope broke during a river crossing and caused the death of one person. Germany lost two students in an avalanche, and Veld and Vlei lost one instructor and two students out of a group of fifty-six people when they were exposed to a sudden devastating change in weather. In another African school, a student fell to his death from the ropes course.

Some of these tragedies were the result of human frailty—disobeying strict instructions, or physiological weakness such as an allergy. Those attributable to "acts of God"—lightning, avalanche, unexpectedly severe weather changes—perhaps could have been averted, but that is hindsight.

All the Outward Bound schools take their responsibility to the people who have come to them very seriously, but they observe safety in different ways. A few use thick manuals that spell everything out in great detail, others train their instructors thoroughly and then leave safety to their good judgement. Over and above that are national safety standards which have been devised by the British Trust, Outward Bound Inc., Outward Bound Canada and other Outward Bound umbrella organizations. Ulf Händel, director of the school at Baad, Germany, has visited most of the schools and suggests that Outward Bound staff from the different countries should meet and discuss safety standards. He is convinced they could all learn from each other and possibly prevent the preventable accidents.

Ironically, Outward Bound's high reputation c...
picion. The glowing rhetoric of its supporters often gives ...
a backlash ("It *can't* be that wonderful"). Another problem is
that Outward Bound lends itself to many interpretations. Tom
Price, former warden of Eskdale, says he can predict the reac-
tions when Outward Bound is mentioned: "Intellectuals
describe it as too hearty, muscular, dangerous and paramilitary.
Nonthinkers consider it sound, like corporal punishment or
compulsory games. The well-off approve of it as the right kind
of discipline for the masses, while the masses condemn it
because it sounds like another way of getting at them, like
religion. Teachers, especially those in physical education,
approve wholeheartedly. Both ex-servicemen and people who
never were on active service wish they were twenty years
younger and could do it too, secretly thinking that Outward
Bound would recapture for them the piping days of war or at
least ROTC. People running mountaineering schools are all for
it because it puts people in mountains, but members of the
Alpine Club are afraid the mountains might be desecrated by
overuse. Some confuse it with detention centres, or a way of
getting boys to wear their hair short."

What then, *is* the essence of Outward Bound?

I believe the answer lies in a phrase with which map makers
of long ago filled in the blank spaces of unexplored regions.
The scholarly wrote, "Terra Incognita," and those with a fanci-
ful mind, "There be Dragons," but the real optimists among
them used the words "More Beyond." Outward Bound gives us
the opportunity to explore the uncharted regions of our body
and our spirit; it is for all of us who are sure that there is More
Beyond.

Appendix

NATIONAL ORGANIZATIONS AND SCHOOLS*

North America

Canadian Outward Bound Mountain School

1600 West 6th Avenue
Vancouver, British Columbia V6J 1R3

school:
P.O. Box 279
Keremeos, British Columbia V0X 1N0

courses:
Summer and winter
Standard from age 16, Senior from age 30
Courses for educators; contract courses for managers, university students, army cadets
Yukon and other expeditions; alpine ski touring
Most programs coeducational

Canadian Outward Bound Wilderness School

36 Madison Avenue
Toronto, Ontario M5R 2S1

school:
P.O. Box 1030
Nipigon, Ontario P0T 2J0

*Course fees have not been provided since they tend to be quickly outdated.

courses:
Summer and winter
Standard from age 16 (17 in winter), Junior from age 14, Adult from
    age 23
Educators from age 21, managers from age 23
River trip from age 18; special rock climbing and whitewater skills
    from age 16
Most programs coeducational

*For general information, posters, pamphlets, reprinted articles and
other literature on Outward Bound in the U.S.:*
Outward Bound, Inc.
384 Field Point Road
Greenwich, Connecticut 06830

Note: U.S. programs are coeducational unless otherwise stated.

Colorado Outward Bound School

945 Pennsylvania Avenue
Denver, Colorado 80203

courses:
Most are mobile
Winter and summer
Standard from age 16½
Special courses for educators, adults from age 30, families with chil-
    dren from age 14
Ski mountaineering, river travel, rock climbing

Dartmouth Outward Bound Center

Dartmouth College
1 College Hall
Hanover, New Hampshire 03755

courses:
On campus: Learning/Living Term
Off campus: skiing, cycling, leadership skills, canoeing
Some courses restricted to Dartmouth College students

Hurricane Island Outward Bound School

P.O. Box 429
Rockland, Maine 04841

courses:
Summer courses in Maine; winter courses in Florida; some winter
  courses on mainland of Maine
Standard from age 16½, Junior from age 15, Adult from age 21

Minnesota Outward Bound School

P.O. Box 250
Long Lake, Minnesota 55356

school:
P.O. Box 450
Ely, Minnesota 55731

courses:
Standard from age 16½, Junior from age 14
Special courses for educators, managers, handicapped
Life Career Renewal, Mobile Canoe Wilderness, Winter Wilderness

North Carolina Outward Bound School

P.O. Box 817
Morganton, North Carolina 28655

courses:
Summer and winter courses at Pisgah National Forest; winter courses
  in Florida
Standard from age 16½, Junior from age 15
Mobile cycling from age 16½; educators, intensive adult from age 22

Northwest Outward Bound School

0110 S.W. Bancroft Street
Portland, Oregon 97201

courses:
All are mobile: Oregon, Washington, Idaho, Canada
Winter and summer

Standard mountaineering and ski mountaineering from age 16½,
Adult from age 21
Educators, managers, professionals from age 21
River travel from age 21

Southwest Outward Bound School

P.O. Box 2840
Santa Fe, New Mexico 87501

courses:
All are mobile: Texas, Arizona, New Mexico
Winter and summer
Standard from age 16½, Junior from age 14
Mountain and canyon expedition, river rafting, desert travel, women's
expeditions

Europe

In Great Britain:
Outward Bound Trust
Avon House
360 Oxford Street
London W1N 9HA

Outward Bound Wales

Aberdovey Centre
Aberdovey Gwynedd LL35 0RA

Rhowniar Centre
Tywyn Gwynedd LL36 9HT

courses:
Standard, Rover and Gateway from age 16; Preliminary from age 10;
Adventure from age 12; Junior and Launcher from age 14; Senior
from age 19; Executive from age 25

Eskdale School

Eskdale Green, Cumbria CA19 1TE

courses:
Standard, Rover and Gateway from age 16; Mountain Leaders from
  age 18; Senior and educators from age 20; Executive from age 25

Ullswater School

Penrith, Cumbria

courses:
As at Eskdale School; also Preliminary from age 10, Junior from age
  14

Loch Eil School

Achdalieu Fort William
Invernesshire, Scotland

courses:
Standard, Gateway, Viking, Skye Trek and Launcher Wayfarer from
  age 16; Junior, Sailing and Canoeing from age 14; Functional
  Leadership from age 17; Mountain Leaders from age 18; Yacht-
  master/Coastal from age 18; Senior from age 20; Executive from
  age 25

City Challenge

Canal House
Drapers Field
Coventry, West Midlands CV1 4LG

courses:
Held in York, Humberside, London and other urban centres
Young men and women from age 17

British Army Outward Bound has one centre in Wales, another in
  Norway.

In West Germany:

Deutsche Gesellschaft für Europäische Erziehung
Brienner Strasse 13
8000 München 2

Outward Bound Kurzschule Baad (West Germany)

Kleinwalsertal
8986 Mittelberg-Baad, Austria

courses:
Winter and summer
Young men and women from age 16

Outward Bound Kurzschule Berchtesgaden

Anzenbach 37
8240 Berchtesgaden, West Germany

courses:
Same as Kurzschule Baad's

Landelijke Vereiniging, Outward Bound School VZW

B–3030 Heverlee
Tervuurse Vest 101, Belgium

courses:
One week for young people; two to three days for executives

Zee en Bergscholen in Nederland

Huize Anneville
Ulvenhout (NB)
Postbus 44
Annevillan 101, Netherlands

courses:
Standard for boys and girls from age 15; Senior from age 24

Africa

Outward Bound Trust of Kenya

P.O. Box 49576
Nairobi, Kenya

school:
Outward Bound Mountain School
P.O. Box 10
Loitokitok, Kenya

Course information unavailable

Outward Bound Trust of Tanzania

Directorate of Sports and Youth
Coronation House
P.O. Box 4284
Dar es Salaam, Tanzania

courses:
Standard for secondary school boys; Senior for young men in business
    and industry; Girls' and Young Women's for students and working
    women

Outward Bound Association of Lesotho

P.O. Box 61587
Marshalltown 2107, South Africa

school:
Thaba Phatsoa Outward Bound Centre
P.O. Box 367
Leribe, Lesotho

courses:
Standard for men and women from age 16; Junior for boys and girls
    from age 14; Executive for adults

Asia

Outward Bound Trust of Malaysia

P.O. Box 295
52 Ampang Road
Kuala Lumpur, Malaysia

school:
Telok Batik
Lumut, Perak, Malaysia

courses:
Standard for men ages 18 to 25; Women's for ages 18 to 25
Ten 25-day courses per year

Singapore Outward Bound School

c/o Ministry of Defence
No. 2, SAF Club
Beach Road
Singapore 0718

school:
Pulau Ubin

courses:
Standard for men ages 15 to 30; Women's for ages 15 to 30; Junior
  Boys and Girls for ages 15 to 20; Executive for adults

Outward Bound Trust of Hong Kong

P.O. Box 36
Hong Kong

courses:
Standard for men from age 18; Junior for boys and girls from age 7
Special courses for girls, adults and handicapped; weekend programs
  for families

Australia and New Zealand

Outward Bound Australia

453 Kent Street
Box 4213 GPO
Sydney 2000, New South Wales

school:
c/o Post Office
Tharwa, A.C.T.

courses:
Held in New South Wales and Queensland
Standard for men and women from age 17; Adult for men and
women from age 30; Pack and Paddle from age 12
Special courses for organizations, schools, educators

Outward Bound South Australia

Box 1590 GPO
Adelaide, South Australia 5001

school:
P.O. Box 51
Milang, South Australia

courses:
Standard for men and women from age 17; Junior for boys and girls
from age 14½; Senior for adults
Special courses for school groups from age 14½, instructors and sponsors

Outward Bound Trust of New Zealand

P.O. Box 3158
Wellington, New Zealand

school:
Cobham Outward Bound School
Anakiwa
Private Bag Picton, New Zealand

courses:
Standard for men from age 17, for women from age 17; Adult from
age 30
Special short courses for mentally handicapped

"NOT QUITE BLOOD RELATIONS"

Citizenship and Leadership Centre

61 Broad Street
P.O. Box 1171
Lagos, Nigeria

schools:
Mountain School
Shere Hills
P.O. Box 676
Jos, Nigeria

Sea School
Apapa BMP 1187, Nigeria

Aluu Temporary Centre
Port Harcourt, Nigeria

courses:
A large number and variety are offered at all centres, which include a
    Women's Unit and a Mobile Unit
Junior from age 12, Intermediate from age 15, Senior and Executive
    from age 21
Special courses for students of physical and health education; school
    prefects; the uniformed services; Man O'War Clubs; civil service
Coeducational; men only; women only

Veld and Vlei Adventure Trust

517 Allied Building
93 Main Street
Port Elizabeth, South Africa

courses:
Winter and summer during school holidays
At Estcourt, Natal; Elgin (near Cape Town) and Sedgefield (near
    Knysna), Cape Province
For men and women from age 16

Hawaii Bound

Room 220
825 Keeaumaku Street
Honolulu, Hawaii 96814

school:
P.O. Box 207
Kamuela, Hawaii 96743

courses:
Standard for men and women from age 16, Junior for boys and girls
from age 12
Special courses for adults, women, families, couples, educators, youth
workers

La Guilde Européenne du Raid

15 Quai de Conti
75006 Paris, France

courses:
Winter and summer
Men and women from age 18

Outward Bound and Adventure Training for the Youth of Bermuda

Police Headquarters
P.O. Box 530
Hamilton 5, Bermuda

courses:
Boys and girls from age 12

Japan Outward Bound

Preparation Committee
Room 422
Sanno Grand Building
14–2 Nagata-Cho
2–Chome, Chiyoda-Ku
Tokyo, Japan

Bibliography

80. Geburtstag: Kurt Hahn; Festreden und Ansprachen. 1966. (Privately printed for Schule Schloss Salem, West Germany.)

Byatt, D.A., comp. *Kurt Hahn: An Appreciation of His Life and Work.* Gordonstoun School, 1976. (Privately printed.)

Fletcher, Basil. *The Challenge of Outward Bound.* London: William Heinemann Ltd., 1971.

Hogan, J.M. *Beyond the Classroom.* Reading: Educational Explorers Ltd., 1970.

———. *Impelled into Experiences: The Story of the Outward Bound Schools.* Wakefield: Educational Productions Ltd., 1968.

Hopkins, David. "Self-Concept and Adventure." Master of Education thesis, Sheffield University, 1976.

James, David, ed. *Outward Bound.* London: Routledge & Kegan Paul Ltd., 1957.

Jeneid, Michael. *Adventuring Outward Bound.* Melbourne: Lansdowne Press, 1967.

Lacey, Robert. *Majesty.* New York: Avon Books, 1977.

Liversidge, Douglas. *Prince Philip, First Gentleman of the Realm.* St. Albans: Panther Books Ltd., 1977.

Richards, Garry E. "Some Educational Implications and Contributions of Outward Bound." Sydney, 1977. (Privately printed.)

Roberts, K.; White, G.E.; and Parker, H.J. *The Character-Training Industry.* Newton Abbot: David & Charles, 1974.

Röhrs, Hermann. *Kurt Hahn: A Life Span in Education and Politics.* London: Routledge & Kegan Paul Ltd., 1970.

Salem, West Germany. Schule Schloss Salem. Speech by Georg Wilhelm of Hanover given at Kurt Hahn's funeral service, 1974.

Shipton, Eric. *Untravelled World.* London: Hodder & Stoughton Ltd., 1969.

Shore, Arnold. *Outward Bound: A Research Volume.* New York: Russell Sage Foundation, 1977.

Index